Discovering Business Gold

Actionable assessment practices for identifying untapped organizational performance improvement opportunities

Wayne,
   Thank you for your advice,
Counsel, and especially your
friendship

   All the Best,
Nathan

6/23/2016

Discovering Business Gold

Actionable assessment practices for identifying untapped organizational performance improvement opportunities

Nathan Ives MBA, PMP

StrategyDriven Enterprises, LLC
2015

First Printing: 2015

ISBN 978-1-329-75522-2

StrategyDriven Enterprises, LLC
1720 Mars Hill Road, Suite 8-232
Acworth, Georgia, USA 30101

www.StrategyDriven.com

Special discounts are available on quantity purchases by corporations, associations, educators, and others. For details, contact the publisher at the above listed address.

U.S. trade bookstores and wholesalers: Please contact StrategyDriven Enterprises, LLC at (678) 810-0892 or via email at ContactUs@StrategyDriven.com.

Printed in the United States of America.

Dedication

To my Mom and Dad, whose love and encouragement inspire me to always be and do my best.

Contents

Forward

"The shortest distance between two points is a straight line."
Archimedes

All of my career, I've been challenged by resource limitations. Quite honestly, I don't know any leader who isn't. And so the difference between success and failure or, at least, the degree to which one is successful lies with how effectively those limited resources are used.

Effective resource use begins with the knowledge of where one's organization is and where it is going as only then can the optimal actions to go from Point A (where one is) to Point B (where one wants to go) be defined.

Business performance assessments answer the question of where one's organization is at (actual performance), provide a sense for where the organization should go (target performance), and help define the actions necessary to make the journey (recommendations).

The quality of assessments and the assessment program, of course, dictates to a great degree at what point on the spectrum of success an organization is able to achieve.

I've had the privilege of leading and participating in dozens of full-scope assessments for companies large and small. Over time, it became apparent which practices resulted in better, more actionable insights and which others diminished assessment effectiveness. ***Discovering Business Gold*** catalogs these decades of learnings so you can benefit from this experience without having to perform dozens of assessments yourself.

Keep in mind that business performance assessments should represent only one component of your organization's evaluation and control program. Equally important is the Management Observation Program, Benchmarking Program, Corrective Action Program, and Organizational Performance Measures Program, all of which serve to inform the Business Performance Assessment Program and further extend post assessment value.

As a part of StrategyDriven's ongoing commitment to performance improvement, we welcome your feedback and questions on *Discovering Business Gold* at DBG@StrategyDriven.com.

Thank you for purchasing *Discovering Business Gold* and may your assessments bring you the insights needed to take your organization to the next level of performance.

All the Best,

Nathan

Nathan Ives
President & Chief Executive Officer
StrategyDriven Enterprises, LLC

Preface

Organizations successfully identifying and resolving their own problems operate more safely, reliably, and efficiently. Business performance assessments represent one method for identifying conditions adverse to quality and opportunities for performance improvement; providing a means for a broad cross-section of employees to become involved in attaining and maintaining the high levels of organizational performance necessary for success. As such, these assessments are an integral part of an organization's commitment to excellence and should be used to continuously improve performance.

The business performance assessment program is based on the following principles:

- The business performance assessment program is formally defined; providing guidance for performing critical, high-quality evaluations
- Business performance assessments measure organizational performance against business objectives, management expectations, high industry standards and best practices, operating experience, and regulatory requirements
- Each business performance assessment focuses on safety, reliability, efficiency, compliance, and risk
- Each organization routinely conducts its own evaluation of people, process, and technology performance
- Independent oversight groups periodically evaluate people, process, and technology performance
- People with the necessary expertise conduct business performance assessment activities
- Assessors are in the field observing important activities whenever possible

- Assessors thoroughly understand key organization events as they relate to the business performance assessment
- Assessment conclusions are founded on facts and logically derived
- An assessment's strength and credibility is derived from the team, not an individual team member
- Those conducting business performance assessments establish a professional relationship and communicate closely with those being assessed to ensure understanding of and ownership for the results
- Management verifies that the issues are promptly entered into the corrective action program for resolution
- Assessment results are communicated to affected groups and individuals
- Organizational business performance assessments are periodically analyzed in aggregate to identify broad cross-functional issues
- Functional area business performance assessments are periodically analyzed in aggregate to identify common underlying performance issues
- Business performance assessment program effectiveness is periodically evaluated and upgraded, as necessary

How to Use this Book

Discovering Business Gold contains the principles, best practices, and warning flags associated with self-critical, value-adding business performance assessments. Rather than reading this book from cover-to-cover, *The Assessment Process* and *Global Principles and Best Practices* chapters should be read first; immediately followed by those principles, best practices, and warning flags associated with each process phase prior to performing those activities during an actual assessment.

Principles, best practices, and warning flags each present unique information to aid in the performance of the business performance assessment process. In general, these categories can be described as:

- ***Principles***: Fundamental activities or performance attributes without which effective performance cannot be achieved. Principles may be embedded within procedures or behavioral standards/expectations. Consequently, principle-based activities or performance should be readily observable.

- ***Best Practices***: Those activities or performance attributes that enhance organizational results. Best practices may be procedurally driven or behaviorally based. Consequently, best practices can be readily observed, recognized, and quantified.

- ***Warning Flags***: Those activities or performance attributes that diminish an organization's effectiveness. By their very nature, warning flags are active, not passive. They may be procedurally driven or behaviorally based. Consequently, warning flags can be readily observed, recognized, and corrected or eliminated.

Each principle, best practice, and warning flag is consistently structured to present quickly referable, immediately actionable information:

- ***First Paragraph***: Statement and description of common issue to be resolved concluding with the practice that addresses the issue (subject of the principle, best practice, or warning flag).

- ***Second Paragraph***: Detailed description of the solution (subject of the principle, best practice, or warning flag).

- ***Third + Paragraph***: High level discussion of how to actionably implement the solution.

- ***Final Thought(s)...*** (Optional): One or more paragraphs providing experience-based commentary on other applications of the solution, warnings, or things to look out for when implementing the solution, etcetera

Introduction

Standard Business Process Overview

A process is a series of actions and decisions used to transform raw inputs into a desired output. Processes may be documented or undocumented. Some are supported by software applications and other technologies. All processes consume resources (land, labor, and/or capital) during their execution.

Organizations function through a collection of often interrelated processes. Well-structured processes use resources efficiently, transfer data seamlessly, are performed consistently, and yield high-value outputs.

The Business Performance Assessment process is a *Control Process* used to manage Operational and Infrastructure processes. It guides the collection, aggregation, and analysis of organizational data to yield actionable performance improvement insights.

The Business Performance Assessment Process presented in **Discovering Business Gold** reflects the practices characteristic of well-structured assessment processes used by leading companies and top-tier consulting firms worldwide. Activity steps are organized as a simple linear progression to guide performance of an insightful performance assessment. When applicable, activity performance principles, best practices, and warning flags are provided. An overview of the entire Business Performance Assessment Process is illustrated by Figures 1a – 1d.

Discovering Business Gold provides all of the information needed to perform objective, self-critical, and insightful business performance assessments. However, should formal process implementation tools (implementing procedures, forms, process performance metrics, and/or supporting software), training, or onsite assessment support be desired, visit: www.StrategyDriven.com/bpap for more information and to sign-up for a no-obligation free consultation.

Business Performance Assessment Program Overview

An integral part of the learning organization's evaluation and control program, the Business Performance Assessment Program provides in-depth evaluations of organizational functions or characteristics for the purpose of identifying improvement opportunities. Business performance assessments are powerful tools deriving their heightened value from the synthesis of information from multiple sources; creating a rich, integrated picture of organizational performance as compared to established standards and marketplace benchmarks. This integrated picture of performance also benefits from the progressive infusion of knowledge and experience applied to the initial interpretation of data used to develop the assessment's source information.

Business performance assessment programs are comprised of scheduled and unscheduled assessments. Because business performance assessments are not performed on a continual basis, they are inappropriate for the monitoring of rapidly changing conditions. Circumstances for which periodic and event driven business performance assessments are performed can be described as:

__Scheduled__

- *__Foundational__*: assessments occurring at a given frequency within a defined time interval typically focused on core business risks, operational goals, and organizational values. These assessments target those critical organizational functions and characteristics that present significant risk, must be performed with precision, or require continuous improvement to maintain marketplace competitiveness

- *Situational:* assessments targeted at specific high-risk activities to ensure risk mitigating behaviors and mechanisms are present during these critical times. These assessments include reviews of the integrated training, execution, and follow-up improvements associated with these events

Unscheduled

- *Event-based*: assessments performed after a significant performance expectation violation that sets a dangerous precedent or causes significantly adverse impacts to the organization. The assessments scans a broad number of organizational groups, especially those performing similar operations to that group in which the violation occurred, so to identify the extent of condition of the undesired deviation and to broadly reinforce adherence to proper management standards. Note that the business performance assessment and corrective action programs should also be examined to determine why precursor deviations were not identified and corrective action taken prior to the event's occurrence

- *Random:* assessments reinforcing desired behaviors performed at the discretion of the business performance assessment program manager and/or senior organization leaders. Such random assessments reinforce with employees the need to be ever vigilant to the adherence of workplace standards because their compliance is monitored at all times

Business performance assessments belong to the third tier of performance data refinement. Performance reports at this level benefit from human intelligence added to supporting data during initial data synthesis, basic trend identification and analysis, multi-trend synthesis, and basic model application. It is the infusion of human knowledge and experience at these points that makes business performance assessments broadly integrated and highly insightful.

.

The Assessment Process

Business performance assessments should focus on evaluating the most important aspects of the people, process, and technology performance dimensions comprising the area being evaluated. They are comprehensive performance evaluations based on a collection of observations, record reviews, personnel interviews, benchmarking data, and other ongoing assessment information measured against specific criteria. Assessments identify performance deficiencies and their potential causes in addition to areas of strength and opportunities for improvement.

Effective business performance assessments evaluate performance against established performance goals and standards, industry best practices, and regulatory requirements. Foundational assessments are performed on a recurring basis, situational assessments target specific high-risk activities, event-based assessments are performed in response to significant expectation violations and random assessments reinforce desired behaviors.

Roles and Responsibilities

Effective implementation of business performance assessments requires clear definition of participant roles and responsibilities. These definitions delineate the lines of communications, decision authority, and activity obligations of key positions involved with each assessment including the:

- Executive Sponsor
- Business Performance Assessment Team Leader

Discovering Business Gold

- Business Performance Assessment Team Member
- Business Performance Assessment Stakeholders
- All Personnel

Executive Sponsor

The Executive Sponsor oversees the direction and activities of the business performance assessment team. This individual is typically an executive or senior manager who is knowledgeable of but not necessarily responsible for the operations/activities being assessed. The Executive Sponsor should possess good working relationships and be respected by his/her peers throughout the organization. Executive Sponsor responsibilities often include but are not limited to:

- Providing overall perspective and direction for the business performance assessment thereby ensuring the evaluation's alignment with organization's vision, mission, values, and goals;
- Approving the business performance assessment's scope and objectives including in-progress changes;
- Garnering organizational support for the performance of the business performance assessment;
- Ensuring the Business Performance Assessment Team Leader has access to the personnel, material, financial, and information resources needed to effectively perform the business performance assessment;
- Confirming overall business performance assessment staffing and team members;
- Challenging the business performance assessment team's findings so to guarantee their validity and organizational value;
- Communicating the business performance assessment's findings with senior executives, managers, and board members, as needed;

- Supporting the Business Performance Assessment Team Leader in the resolution of conflicts outside of his/her authority; and
- Approving the final business performance assessment report thereby committing the organization to implementing identified follow-on corrective actions

Business Performance Assessment Team Leader

The Business Performance Assessment Team Leader is the individual responsible for the quality and timely performance of the specifically assigned business performance assessment. This individual possesses the leadership and managerial skills necessary to effectively direct the business performance assessment team in the performance of its work. The Business Performance Assessment Team Leader's responsibilities often include but are not limited to:

- Focusing the business performance assessment team on the specified assessment objectives;
- Creating the business performance assessment plan and activity schedule;
- Identifying and requesting personnel, material, financial, and information resources needed to effectively perform the business performance assessment;
- Deploying assigned business performance assessment resources to best meet the specified assessment objectives;
- Developing clear and concise, objective and critical beneficial practices, performance shortfalls, and overall business performance assessment report;
- Providing timely communications to the Executive Sponsor, Business Performance Assessment Team Members, and Business Performance Assessment Stakeholders;

Discovering Business Gold

- Identifying, communicating, monitoring, and responding to risks; and
- Managing the scope, schedule, cost, and quality constraints associated with the assigned business performance assessment

Business Performance Assessment Team Member

The Business Performance Assessment Team Members are individuals who carry out the work but who are not necessarily involved with management of the business performance assessment. The team is comprised of individuals from different work groups possessing the specific knowledge, skills, and experiences necessary to objectively and critically evaluate the subject performance. Responsibilities of Business Performance Assessment Team Members often include but are not limited to:

- Supporting the Business Performance Assessment Team Leader in the performance of his/her duties;
- Reviewing policies, procedures, and standards against known best practices;
- Analyzing performance data to identify whether performance exceeds, meets, or falls short of established standards;
- Interviewing key activity stakeholders for understanding, reinforcement, and compliance with performance expectations;
- Observing activity execution for compliance with performance standards;
- Synthesizing gathered performance data into objective, critical beneficial practices and performance shortfalls
- Clearly and concisely documenting performance observations, beneficial practices, performance shortfalls, and the overall business performance assessment report; and

- Processing identified deficiencies within the corrective action program for follow-up and resolution

Business Performance Assessment Stakeholders

Business Performance Assessment Stakeholders are those individuals or organizations who are actively involved in the business performance assessment or whose interests may be influenced by the assessment's positive and/or negative findings. Stakeholders may be internal and/or external to the organization and exert influence over the assessment, its findings, and team members.

While all of the aforementioned business performance assessment participants are stakeholders, Business Performance Assessment Stakeholders refers to those executives and functional area managers responsible for the performance being assessed. These individuals include those responsible for overseeing (executives), directing (managers and supervisors), and performing (individual contributors / workers) the activities; processes, procedures, and standards; technology; and organization design under evaluation. Business Performance Assessment Stakeholders responsibilities typically include but are not limited to:

All

- Providing local perspective and technical input to the business performance assessment team;
- Supporting activity observations and personnel interviews; and
- Responding to surveys

Discovering Business Gold

First-line Executives

- Receiving, challenging, and understanding the business performance assessment team's conclusions;
- Ensuring business performance assessment results and follow-up actions are shared with direct reports; and
- Overseeing the resolution of identified performance shortfalls and promulgation of beneficial practices

Second-line Managers (commonly Functional Area Managers)

- Validating the business performance assessment team's observation facts;
- Recommending additional data sources supporting the business performance assessment team's evaluation efforts;
- Receiving, challenging, and understanding the business performance assessment team's conclusions;
- Owning and resolving identified performance shortfalls;
- Ensuring business performance assessment results and follow-up actions which are shared with direct reports; and
- Sharing identified beneficial practices across the organization

All Personnel

All Personnel are responsible for:

- Applying the principles of business performance assessment in their daily activities;
- Documenting conditions adverse to quality, areas for improvement, enhancements, and recommendations, in accordance with the corrective actions program; and

- Performing required follow-up activities, discovered during a business performance, assessment in accordance with the operating standards and corrective action program guidelines

Assessment Phases

Business performance assessments are conducted in a series of phases: Identify, Plan & Schedule, Execute, and Close-out. Associated with each phase is a collection of principles, best practices, and warning flags aiding the identification, communication, and acceptance of value-adding, self-critical performance improvement opportunities.

Complimenting these phase-based approaches are a collection of global principles and best practices that apply throughout the assessment process. Global principles and best practices include:

Global Principles

- Essential Supporting Behaviors
- Use of Experience

Global Best Practices

- Documented Business Performance Assessment Program
- Periodic Assessment of the Business Performance Assessment Program

Identify Phase

The *Identify Phase* starts the business performance assessment process by defining the broad parameters within and by which the assessment will be performed. Activities comprising the *Identify Phase* include (See Figure 1a, Identify Phase):

- ***Step 1, Select the Assessment to be Performed***: Identify the assessment to be performed from the organization's Business Performance Assessment Schedule. At this point in the process, the business performance assessment is generally defined as a topical area to be evaluated.

  Proper assessment selection optimizes the value realized by the organization. All assessments have associated time and personnel costs, therefore, it is important to select those areas representing the highest improvement potential for evaluation.

  The following best practices guide optimal assessment selection:
  - Integrated Risk Assurance Oversight Matrix
  - Identify Risk-based Business Performance Assessments
  - Foundational, Situational, Event-based, & Random Observations
  - Random, Unannounced Inspections
  - Assessment Calendars

- ***Step 2, Define the Assessment Scope and Approach***: The assessment scope and approach are defined by identifying the specific people, processes, and technologies to be evaluated as well as the methods of evaluation.

  Defining an assessment's specific scope and approach can be as important as selecting the assessment topic. A scope that is too broad commonly yields shallow performance improvement insights and consumes excessive resources. A scope that is too narrow limits the identification of performance improvement opportunities reducing overall assessment value.

When defining an assessment's scope, the following parameters should be specified:
1. Functional area(s) / Assessment topic
2. Risk(s) to be addressed
3. Reason for conducting the assessment
4. SMART assessment objectives
5. Applicable organizational goals and internal standards, processes, and procedures
6. Applicable industry practices and regulatory requirements
7. Period to be assessed
8. Assessment performance timing

An assessment approach ill-suited to management objectives limits insights gained and overall value. The error here is one of focus where the acquisition of broad or deep understanding is desired but not achieved.

The following principles guide optimal assessment approach selection:
- The Vertical Slice Approach
- The Horizontal Cut Approach
- Combination Assessment Approach

- **Step 3, *Assign the Assessment Team*:** The assessment's executive sponsor, team leader and team members are assigned based on their qualifications relative to the assessment's scope and evaluation approach.

An assessment's overall quality is largely driven by the knowledge, skills, and experiences of the assessment team members. Thus, their selection is critical to the assessment process.

When selecting an assessment Team Leader and Team Members, consider the following factors:

1. Does the individual have the requisite technical expertise in the evaluation area to fully understand the underlying regulations, standards, procedures, and technologies?
2. Does the individual have experience in interviewing?
3. Does the individual have experience observing, documenting, and analyzing process performance (people, process, and technology performance attributes)?
4. Does the individual have data analytics experience of the type needed for this assessment?
5. Has the individual performed this or a similar business performance assessment before?
6. Has the individual's supervisor been notified of his/her requested participation?

The following best practices provide additional factors to consider when selecting assessment team participants:

- Executive Sponsorship
- Multidiscipline Teams
- Seek Local Participation for Context
- Independent Assessors
- *advocatus diaboli* – The Devil's Advocate

Plan & Schedule Phase

The business performance assessment process continues with the *Plan & Schedule Phase* during which the specific assessment activities –

document reviews, personnel surveys, activity observations, and individual interviews – to be performed are identified and scheduled. Activities comprising the *Plan & Schedule Phase* include (See Figure 1b, Plan & Schedule Phase):

- ***Step 4, Identify Assessment Focus Areas*:** Identify the several performance areas (people, processes, and technologies) to be focused on during the assessment based on a review of the preliminary data and the assessment's scope and objectives.

  Until this point, the assessment's scope has been broadly defined based on organizational risks and executive level performance metrics. Identifying specific focus areas involves a review of preliminary workgroup level performance including prior assessment reports, workgroup performance metrics, and workgroup events including causal analysis and corrective action documents. Refining the assessment's scope into a few select focus areas further ensures valuable performance improvement insights are revealed.

  The following beneficial practice and warning flag are associated with identifying an assessment's focus areas:
  - Assess the Good, the Bad, and the Ugly
  - Inwardly Focused Performance Assessments

- ***Step 5, Develop Assessment Plan*:** Develop a detailed assessment plan to efficiently guide team member activities throughout the evaluation. Such plans coordinate team member activities so to eliminate redundancy and maximize information sharing by creating an awareness of what each participant is doing. Effective assessment plans include the following information:

- – Assessment scope and objectives
- – Performance criteria
- – Major activity milestone timeline
- – Personnel resources
- – Past area performance history
- – Related events since the last area assessment
- – Prioritized assessment focus areas
- – Observations (document and data reviews, personnel surveys, activity observations, and personnel interviews) to be performed

- **_Step 6, Develop Assessment Schedule_**: Develop a detailed, daily assessment schedule of the activities to be performed; identifying individual(s) responsible, objectives and criteria to be satisfied, and location of performance.

Effective schedules communicate the 'when' of activity performance; enabling team members to coordinate information and observation gathering needs, particularly for follow-up activities, further reducing the redundancy of effort. Such coordination also reduced the team's overall impact on the organization being assessed by minimizing the number of requested interactions intruding on the line organization's productive time.

Execute Phase

The _Execute Phase_ is at the center of the business performance assessment process. During this phase, assessors gather and analyze data from a number of sources to identify performance improvement opportunities. Activities comprising the _Execute Phase_ include (See Figure 1c.1, Execute Phase, part 1 and Figure 1c.2, Execute Phase, part 2):

- *Step 7, Gather Data*: Gather document, data, survey, activity, and interview facts including:

Document and Data Facts

- Standards and Policy Documents
- Procedures
- Logs and Records
- Metrics
- Past Business Performance Assessments
- Root Cause, Apparent Cause, and Direct Cause Assessments
- Condition/Trouble Reports
- Management Observation Program Data
- External Performance Evaluation Reports
- Regulatory Findings
- Benchmarking Reports
- Internal and External Operating Experience
- Relevant supporting software application data

Survey Facts

- Quantitative survey questions counts
- Qualitative survey question answers

Activity Facts

Assessor identified objective, unbiased observation facts including:

- Programs (standards and expectations, procedures, schedules, etcetera)
- Jobsite Conditions (cleanliness, distractions, ergonomics, etcetera)

    – Individual Behaviors (actions/performance, behaviors, decisions, communications, etcetera)

Interview Facts

Assessor collected objective, unbiased interview statements regarding:
- Interviewee perspectives on programmatic/positional roles and responsibilities, why decisions were made and/or actions taken, and local context and historical perspective as related to
  - Programs (standards and expectations, procedures, schedules, etcetera)
  - Jobsite Conditions (cleanliness, distractions, ergonomics, etcetera)
  - Individual Behaviors (actions/performance, behaviors, decisions, communications, etcetera)

The following best practices guide the effective collection of assessment data:
- Observation Announcement Timing
- Use of Standard Observation Forms
- Documented and Signed Observations

- **Step 8, Document Facts**: Formally document objective, unbiased facts obtained from document and data reviews, quantitative and qualitative personnel surveys, activity observations, and personnel interviews.

Each collection of facts, an Observation, should include the following data:
- Facility name

- Date of the observation
- Participating Team members
- Observation title
- Observation scope
- Observation facts / Interview responses:
  - Specific description of the document reviewed including section and/or step number(s) and noteworthy positive and negative characteristics, features, and instructions
  - Specific description of the data reviewed including its source and noteworthy characteristics and analytical results
  - Specific description of the survey issued and noteworthy quantitative and qualitative results
  - Specific description of the activity (function, evolution, briefing, meeting, etcetera) observed and noteworthy positive and negative jobsite conditions, and performance behaviors
  - Questions asked of interviewee (executive, manager, supervisor, or individual contributor) or group and responses received
- Follow-up items
- Observation conclusions

- ***Step 9, Develop Initial Conclusions***: Develop initial finding conclusions and their associated causes, contributors, and insights.

Findings can be either beneficial practices or performance shortfalls. Each conclusion documented should include the following:

Beneficial Practice

- Facility name

Discovering Business Gold

- Functional area
- Assessor
- Factual basis
- Beneficial practice statement

Performance Shortfall

- Facility name
- Functional area assessed
- Functional area impacted
- Assessor
- Factual basis
- Performance shortfall statement
- Actual and potential consequences
- Causes and contributors
- Other insights

Developing self-critical, objective, and value-adding findings is often, the most difficult aspect of a business performance assessment. Numerous logic traps, management pushback, and personal bias can limit a finding's value or worse, make it harmful to the organization.

The following principles, best practices and warning flags guide high-quality assessment finding identification:
- Yellow Sticky Analysis
- Criticisms Appear Harsher When Put Into Print
- Different is not Necessarily Wrong
- Data Synthesis
- Identify Data Relationships
- The Use of Models

- Diverse Models
- Validate the Extremes
- Integrity Without Excuses
- Measure Against Excellence
- Define Issue Materiality
- Three Whys Deep
- Identify the Hidden Drivers, part 1
- Identify the Hidden Drivers, part 2
- Avoid Using Absolutes
- The Illusion of Accuracy
- Using Data as Information
- Absence of Evidence as Evidence of Absence
- Distinction Without a Difference
- Intellectually Empty Assertions
- Massaging the Message for the Boss
- The Normalcy Bias
- Crediting Good Intentions
- Effort Bias
- Conclusion Bias
- Content Without Context
- Distinction Without a Difference

- ***Step 10, Draft Assessment Report*:** Develop the draft business performance assessment report; providing assessment background, participation, and findings.

Assessment reports serve multiple audiences. As such, they should contain an executive level summary and management level response details. Effective assessment reports commonly contain the following sectional details:

Executive Summary

- Summary of key findings
  - Beneficial practices
  - Performance shortfalls
- Immediate actions taken
- Assessment participants
- Facility / Organization participants
- References
- Approvals

Management Level Details

- Beneficial practice forms
- Performance shortfall forms
- Observation forms

The following best practices further support development of high-quality assessment reports:
- Show It Visually
- Separate Fact from Opinion
- Avoid Jargon

- ***Step 11, Conduct Exit Meeting***: Conduct the assessment exit meeting; briefing functional area executives on the assessment's findings and their causes, contributors, and insights.

To ensure optimal engagement and conclusion understanding, at a minimum, the following individuals should attend the Exit Meeting:

- Executive sponsor
- Team leader
- Team members
- Executive responsible for the functional area assessed
- Affected functional area managers

The Exit Meeting should be an interactive discussion between team members and those responsible for the performance assessed. A common Exit Meeting agenda includes:
- Meeting participant introductions
- Assessment results summary discussion
- Management response/actions planned to resolve assessment findings
- Report distribution timing
- Assessment follow-up actions

The following best practices guide optimal performance of the Exit Meeting:
- Who's on First?
- Don't Break the Mirror

Close-out Phase

The *Close-out Phase* marks the end of the business performance assessment process. Performance improvement opportunities are captured within the corrective action program and assessment documentation is properly cataloged. Activities comprising the *Close-out Phase* include (See Figure 1d, Close-out Phase):

- ***Step 12, Document Improvement Opportunities***: Capture assessment identified deficiencies for corrective action and performance trending within the organization's Corrective Action Program.

This step helps ensure the value of identified performance improvement opportunities are realized by the organization in a timeframe commensurate with the organization's other priorities and available resources. Additional information associated with this step is available in best practice:
- Capture Improvement Opportunities within the Corrective Action Program

- **Step 13, *Close-out Assessment Documentation*:** Finalize and file the business performance assessment report and associated documentation.

This step ensures the information learned during the assessment related to both the organization's performance and the assessment process itself is properly captured for future use. Activities performed during this step include:
- Final assessment report approval
- Assessment report and evidence document filing
- Assessment report grading
- Team leader performance grading and feedback
- Team member performance grading and feedback
- Assessment resources released
- Obligations paid
- Work orders closed

The following best practice and warning flag guide assessment document close-out:
- Training, Grading, and Quality Assessments
- Identifying Mostly Strengths

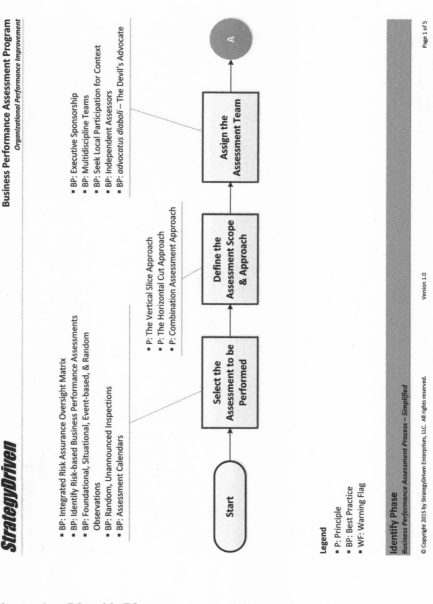

StrategyDriven

Business Performance Assessment Program
Organizational Performance Improvement

- BP: Integrated Risk Assurance Oversight Matrix
- BP: Identify Risk-based Business Performance Assessments
- BP: Foundational, Situational, Event-based, & Random Observations
- BP: Random, Unannounced Inspections
- BP: Assessment Calendars

- P: The Vertical Slice Approach
- P: The Horizontal Cut Approach
- P: Combination Assessment Approach

- BP: Executive Sponsorship
- BP: Multidiscipline Teams
- BP: Seek Local Participation for Context
- BP: Independent Assessors
- BP: *advocatus diaboli* – The Devil's Advocate

Start

Select the Assessment to be Performed

Define the Assessment Scope & Approach

Assign the Assessment Team

A

Legend
- P: Principle
- BP: Best Practice
- WF: Warning Flag

Identify Phase
Business Performance Assessment Process – Simplified

Version 1.0

Page 1 of 5

Figure 1a: *Identify Phase*

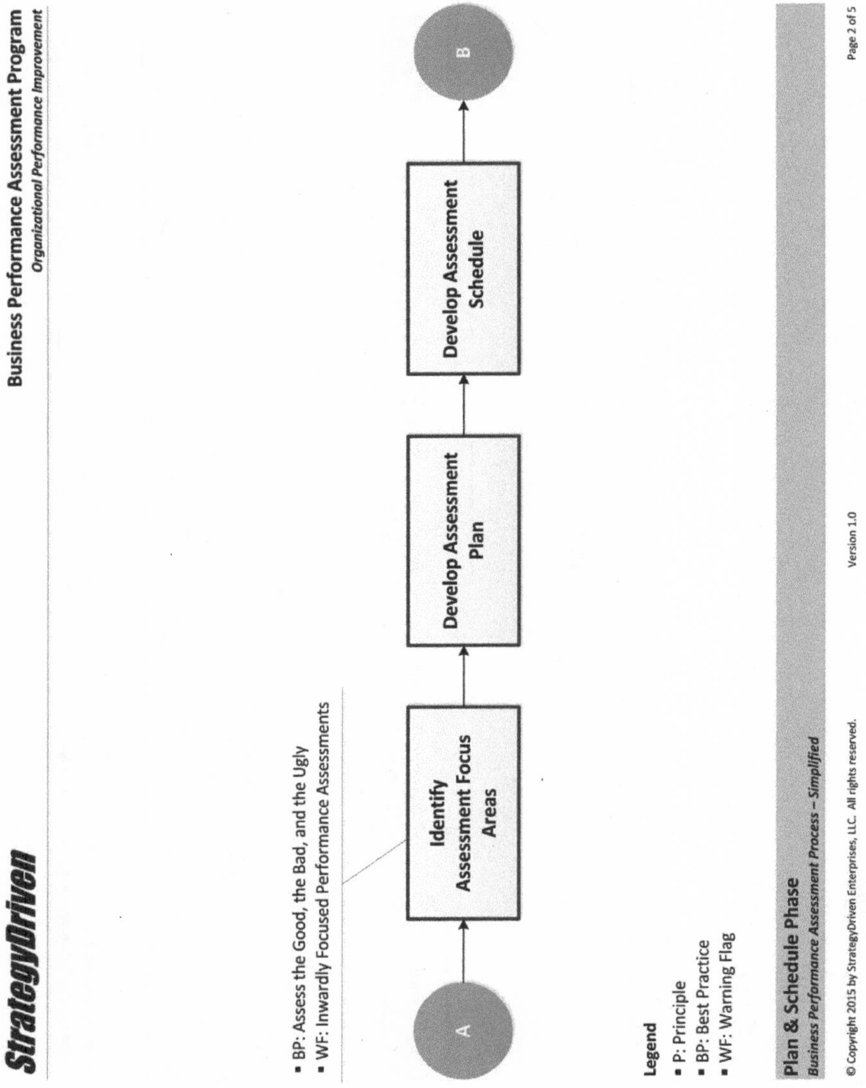

Discovering Business Gold

- BP: Assess the Good, the Bad, and the Ugly
- WF: Inwardly Focused Performance Assessments

A

Identify
Assessment Focus
Areas

Develop Assessment
Plan

Develop Assessment
Schedule

B

Legend
- P: Principle
- BP: Best Practice
- WF: Warning Flag

Plan & Schedule Phase
Business Performance Assessment Process – Simplified

Version 1.0

Figure 1b: *Plan & Schedule Phase*

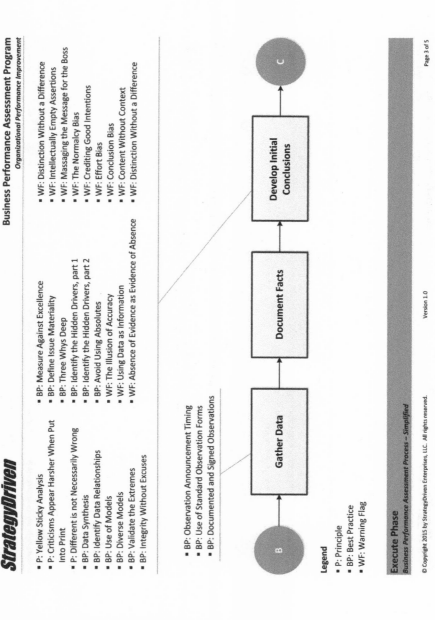

Business Performance Assessment Program
Organizational Performance Improvement

StrategyDriven

- P: Yellow Sticky Analysis
- P: Criticisms Appear Harsher When Put Into Print
- P: Different is not Necessarily Wrong
- BP: Data Synthesis
- BP: Identify Data Relationships
- BP: Use of Models
- BP: Diverse Models
- BP: Validate the Extremes
- BP: Integrity Without Excuses

- BP: Measure Against Excellence
- BP: Define Issue Materiality
- BP: Three Whys Deep
- BP: Identify the Hidden Drivers, part 1
- BP: Identify the Hidden Drivers, part 2
- BP: Avoid Using Absolutes
- WF: The Illusion of Accuracy
- WF: Using Data as Information
- WF: Absence of Evidence as Evidence of Absence

- WF: Distinction Without a Difference
- WF: Intellectually Empty Assertions
- WF: Massaging the Message for the Boss
- WF: The Normalcy Bias
- WF: Crediting Good Intentions
- WF: Effort Bias
- WF: Conclusion Bias
- WF: Content Without Context
- WF: Distinction Without a Difference

- BP: Observation Announcement Timing
- BP: Use of Standard Observation Forms
- BP: Documented and Signed Observations

B → **Gather Data** → **Document Facts** → **Develop Initial Conclusions** → **C**

Legend
- P: Principle
- BP: Best Practice
- WF: Warning Flag

Execute Phase
Business Performance Assessment Process – Simplified

© Copyright 2015 by StrategyDriven Enterprises, LLC. All rights reserved.

Version 1.0

Page 3 of 5

Figure 1c.1: Execute Phase, part 1

Discovering Business Gold

Figure 1c.2: Execute Phase, part 2

Page | 24

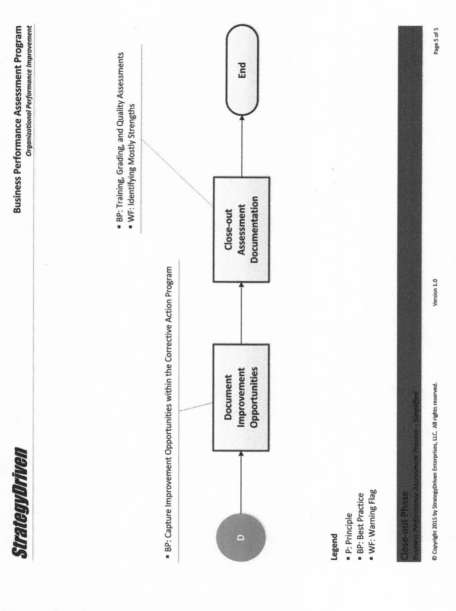

Figure 1d: Close-out Phase

Global Principles and Best Practices

Effective business performance assessment programs result in critical, constructive, credible, and consistent evaluations from which performance improvement actions are derived. Achieving this level of performance necessitates the application of a core set of supporting behaviors and best practices.

The following principles and best practices elaborate on those core elements necessary for consistently superior business performance assessment program performance.

Global Principles

- Essential Supporting Behaviors
- Use of Experience

Global Best Practices

- Documented Business Performance Assessment Program
- Periodic Assessment of the Business Performance Assessment Program

Global Principles

Essential Supporting Behaviors

Effective evaluation and control programs rely on a set of underlying behaviors promoting continuous performance improvement. While positionally dependent, these behaviors foster the continuous identification and resolution of performance improvement opportunities and shortfalls.

Individual performance improvement behaviors vary across a spectrum based on organizational position. Executives and senior manager promote a culture of continuous improvement while individual contributors challenge underlying assumptions and practices and resist complacency. The following lists provide illustrative examples of the continuous performance improvement behaviors exhibited by individuals at all organizational levels supporting effective evaluation and control programs.

Executives and Senior Managers (Directors, Vice Presidents, and Above)

- Challenge managers, supervisors, and staff to continually improve performance relative to the organization's vision, mission, values, and goals
- Align evaluation and control programs with the organization's vision, mission, values, and goals
- Establish goals, define and reinforce standards, make decisions, and communicate support for ongoing improvement opportunity / problem identification and implementation / resolution

- Reinforce with managers the need for and value of continuous learning through routine, critical assessments and the systematic incorporation of internal and external lessons learned
- Welcome performance improvement input from all levels of the organization including a demonstration of respect for differing opinions
- Create an environment within which employees readily identify and report performance issues that are subsequently resolved in a timely manner commensurate with their organizational significance
- Ensure employees feel free to raise performance improvement opportunities and shortfalls without the fear of retribution
- Hold themselves and their subordinates accountable for using evaluation and control programs to identify and close performance gaps
- Emphasize the importance of resolving problems the first time and demonstrate a low tolerance for problem recurrence
- Coach managers to identify the connectivity of seemingly unrelated performance issues and resolving their underlying common causes

Operations and Functional Area Managers (Second-line managers)

- Reward self-critical behaviors and the absence of defensiveness to improving performance
- Support and promote participation in business performance assessments and the corrective action program
- Assign personnel with the knowledge, skills, and experiences to effectively execution the evaluation and control programs under their purview
- Challenge evaluation and control program / activity participants to identify objective, critical, and insightful improvement opportunities

- Drive the analysis of performance improvement opportunities / problems to a depth commensurate with the issue's significance
- Routinely communicate evaluation and control program findings to subordinates
- Demonstrate ownership for the timely closure of performance gaps by prioritizing, staffing/funding, and directing activities to effectively improve performance
- Embed performance improvement identification features within organizational processes, procedures, and technologies

Superintendents and Supervisors (First-line managers)

- Recognize self-critical behaviors and the absence of defensiveness to improving performance
- Participate in business performance assessment activities to identify performance improvement opportunities and shortfalls
- Own corrective actions to resolve performance gaps
- Involve subordinates in performance improvement activities

Individual Contributors (Workforce and Staff)

- Proactively observe operations, continually challenge underlying assumptions and practices, and resist complacency
- Readily identify and promptly report performance issues
- Participate in business performance assessment activities to identify performance improvement opportunities and shortfalls
- Propose actions to improve performance, close gaps, and resolve shortfalls
- Assist in the implementation of corrective actions to resolve performance gaps

Use of Experience

Rigorous business performance assessments rely not only on observable, quantifiable facts but also on the experience of those conducting and participating in the assessments. When properly applied experience accelerates issue identification and deepens contributed insights. Experience, however, should not be represented as fact nor should it be used to as the primary mechanism to combine otherwise unrelated facts when making the case for a performance strength or improvement opportunity.

The Role of Experience in the Business Performance Assessment Process

Applying experience is an important part of an effective assessment. Ways in which experience should be applied include:

- *Identifying Observation Opportunities* – Assessors identify and prioritize observation opportunities based on their past operational experience. Such application, combine with a preliminary fact review (performance metrics, procedures, past assessment reports, condition reports, etcetera), helps ensure those activities most likely to contribute meaningful data to the assessment are observed. Furthermore, operational experience aids in the identification of activities that are at higher risk of performance errors.

- *Identifying Observation Relationships* - Assessors should leverage their experience in preliminarily identifying relationships between facts to identify functional issues and between functional issues to identify overall organizational defects. Once an experience-based associated in made, a logical, fact-based analysis should be performed to prove the relationship actually exists for the observed conditions.

- ***Identifying Potential Causes and Contributors to Investigate*** - Once a logical, factually-based performance conclusion is reached, assessors seek to identify the applicable causes and contributors of the problem by developing and then validating an initial list of experience-based hypothetical causes and contributors. The priority
order of validation is also based on the assessors' past experience. Final report causes and contributors, however, are logically and factually validated and not simply an experience-based list.

General Rule of Thumb

In general, experience should be used as a starting point to identify priority focus areas and relationships; somewhat subjective steps of the assessment process. Follow-up with quantitative observations and logical, fact-based analysis is required to substantiate the experience-based suppositions thereby minimizing the possibility of a data gap and logic error that may lead to otherwise inappropriate conclusions.

Key Components Needed to Apply Experience

Those possessing relevant experience who have also learned how to properly apply their experience tend to recognize far more relationships (robust), faster (efficient) than those who do not possess this background. There are three key factors to consider:

- ***Relevance*** - The experience must be relevant to the work (the assessment in this case) being performed. This is not to suggest that the experience must be exactly aligned to be of benefit, in fact, the opposite is often true. The individual's experience should be functionally (from the same business functional area such as finance, human resources, supply chain, information technology, etcetera) or operationally (possessing the same or similar operating elements such human performance, automation, process structure, etcetera) aligned and either organizationally (from the same organization), industrially (from the same or similar industry), or characteristically (possessing the same or similar operating elements such as regulations, hazards, etcetera) aligned. Possessing one or more different experience sets than those that naturally exist within the organization can yield highly beneficial insights not otherwise available to the organization's leadership team.

- *Application Skill* - The individual must be able to apply his/her experience to the work such that he/she is able to use it to recognize patterns, develop relationships, prioritize activities, etcetera. Applying one's experience to a new data set for the expressed purpose of identifying patterns, relationships, and priorities is a skill that needs to be learned, practiced, and mastered. While some individuals possess an extensive range of experiences, they are simply not able to leverage these to the assessment process. Consequently, the value of this experience goes unrealized.
- *Application Willingness* - The individual must be willing to leverage his/her relevant experience in performance of the work. An employee's engagement and the organization's culture greatly influence this. Some employees are disenfranchised with their organization and some cultures establish an employee's unique knowledge and experience as representing his/her worth. In either case, these employees will not offer to apply their experience to the assessment; robbing it of this value.

If any one of these factors is not met, the assessor's experience will likely contribute very little to the overall assessment.

Preventing the Misapplication of Experience

Care must be taken to challenge assessors who appear to be 'jumping to conclusions' based on their past experiences. While experience helps speed relationship identification and understanding, arriving at a conclusion too quickly can be the sign of an opinion-based, experience derived finding. It is often beneficial to challenge all proposed conclusions with questions including:

- What observations led you to that conclusion?
- Did those observed agree with your account/interpretation of their performance?
- How are these facts logically related?
- What have you done to test the validity of your conclusion?
- What feedback have you received from the manager being assessed?

These types of questions probe and challenge an assessor's thinking and help reveal the inappropriate application of experience to the derivation of assessment findings.

Final Thoughts...

When determining a business performance assessment team's composition, it is important to balance individual knowledge, skills, and experience to optimally review the in-scope performance area. One common mistake leaders make during this process is to equate an individual's age or tenure with his/her experience level. Age simply reflects the amount of time an individual has enjoyed on this earth. Tenure simply reflects the number of days spent working within a particular organization(s). Neither directly equates to an experience level.

Experience should be judged based not only on the amount of time performing a specific task but on the success achieved performing that task under varying circumstances as well as the variety of activities the individual performed or was involved with over time and the success of each of these activities. When considering an individual's experience, leaders need to also evaluate the individual's skill and willingness to leverage his/her experience to advance the work assigned.

Let it also be concluded that an assessment devoid of experience is unlikely to provide the organization the deep, rich insights needed to achieve next level performance. While there are dangers associated with the misapplication of experience, without it an assessment will not reflect the true wisdom needed to be of competitive value.

Global Best Practices

Documented Business Performance Assessment Program

Effective performance improvement programs promote alignment of business operations with the organization's vision, mission, values, and goals. Such programs consistently identify opportunities to improve high value-adding operations and to eliminate low value-adding activities. These programs themselves are highly efficient and capable of producing repeatable results. Documenting the business performance assessment process provides the framework necessary to achieve this level of focused execution consistency.

Components of a Well-Documented Business Performance Assessment Process

Well-documented processes are clear, concise, and comprehensive; easily understood and executed by those participating in its performance. Consequently, the business performance assessment process should contain the following documents:

- *Process Procedure* containing:
    - *Introduction and Overview* describing the business performance assessment process, its role in the organization's overall performance improvement program, and desired outcomes to be achieved
    - *Roles and Responsibilities* listing the obligations, by role, of those individuals participating in the business performance assessment process

- *Precautions and Limitations* listing the risks that may arise during the performance of an assessment and the associated mitigating actions to be taken
- *Procedure* providing step-by-step instructions on how to perform a business performance assessment
- *References* listing supporting documentation, commitments, etcetera
- *Glossary* listing acronyms and terms with associated definitions
- *Exhibits* providing forms and checklists to be used when performing assessments
- **Business Performance Assessment Calendar** typically updated on an annual basis
- **Business Performance Assessment Program Metrics** monitoring overall process execution performance and follow-up improvement activities
- **Business Performance Assessment Program Basis Document** providing detailed program implementation information including:
  - *Program Overview* describing the overarching business performance assessment program, its role in the organization's overall performance improvement program, and desired outcomes to be achieved
  - *Program Maturity Model* revealing the performance characteristics of a business performance assessment program across five sequential maturity dimensions
  - *Roles & Responsibilities* listing the obligations, by role, of those individuals participating in the business performance assessment program
  - *Global Principles, Best Practices, and Warning Flags* applying across the program as a whole

- *Program Performance Measures* including definitions
- *Process Flowchart* showing activity-by-activity flow of the business performance assessment process including its interrelationship with other programs
- *Process Flowchart Functional Description* providing the underlying performance details associated with each program activity
- *Activity Principles, Best Practices, and Warning Flags* applying to an individual program activity or group of activities
- *Forms and Checklists* including use instructions
- *Data Synthesis and Analysis Models* including use instructions
- *Glossary* listing acronyms and terms with associated definitions
- **Business Performance Assessment Training Program** for team leaders and members

Final Thought...

In our experience, it is the function of the Business Performance Assessment Program Manager to oversee the development, training, implementation, and maintenance of these documents. Centralizing responsibility for the program in this way further contributes to the consistent performance of individual business performance assessments.

Continuous Monitoring and Periodic Assessment

The value derived from performing business performance assessments directly correlates to the effectiveness of the program itself. In order to maximize its value, the assessment program must be efficiently administered, the individual assessments insightful, and the follow-on improvements recommendations actually implemented. Shortfalls in any of these aspects diminish the program's overall return on investment. Therefore, organization leaders should ensure the assessment program is optimally executed much like the business performance assessment program helps ensure effective, efficient execution of the organization's other activities.

Continuous monitoring and periodic assessment of the business performance assessment program drives ongoing improvements to optimize performance. Effective program oversight consists of both ongoing performance measurement and periodic assessment.

Continuous Performance Measurement and Monitoring

Ongoing performance measurement provides leaders with quantitative feedback regarding the program's execution efficiency. Such measures should be included as a part of the organization's overall performance measurement system and monitored on a monthly or more frequent basis. Common program performance measures include:

- Business Performance Assessments Performed, Overdue, and Deferred
- Business Performance Assessment Corrective Action Backlog, Average Age, Overdue, Closed with No Actions Taken
- Average Business Performance Assessment Grade

Discovering Business Gold

- Issues Identified by External Organizations
- Qualified Business Performance Assessment Team Leaders and Members

In addition to these programmatic performance measures, routine qualitative surveys should also be used to provide continuous performance assessments. Such surveys include:

- Business Performance Assessment Executive Sponsor, Team Leader and Team Members critiques of each assessment performance
- First-line Executive and Second-line Manager post-assessment feedback

Deviations from desired performance levels should be clearly documented including owners, actions, and due dates for resolution.

Periodic Performance Assessment

Periodic, full-scope performance assessments of the business performance assessment program should be conducted by an independent internal oversight group or external organization to ensure program effectiveness. At a minimum, these independent groups should evaluate the assessment program across the following dimensions:

- Evaluation of business performance assessment asserted best practices against those benchmarked by the independent assessors
- Comparison of assessment findings against associated organizational performance measures and ongoing management observations

- Assessment of the implementation timeliness of assessment recommended improvement activities
- Determination of whether or not the desired operational results were achieved following the implementation of assessment recommended improvement activities
- Identification of issue recurrences following the accepted completion of an assessment's recommended improvement actions
- Examination of assessment focus areas versus those areas of greatest operational, financial, regulatory, and reputational risk
- Review of the end-to-end business performance assessment program execution efficiency

These periodic business performance assessment program reviews should be documented, communicated, and followed-up in the manner prescribed by the assessment program itself. Ownership of the associated performance improvement initiatives should be assigned to an executive outside of the business performance assessment program's chain-of-command so to eliminate potential conflicts of interest.

Phase-based Principles, Best Practices, and Warning Flags

Effective business performance assessments provide critical, constructive, credible, and consistent evaluations from which performance improvement actions are derived. Achieving this level of performance necessitates the application of a core set of assessment supporting behaviors and approaches while avoiding those potentially diminishing the assessment's value.

The following principles and best practices elaborate on those core elements necessary for consistently superior assessment performance. The accompanying warning flags highlight those behaviors and approaches that should be avoided so to optimize each assessment's value.

Phase-based Principles

- The Vertical Slide Approach
- The Horizontal Cut Approach
- Combination Assessment Approach
- Yellow Sticky Analysis
- Criticisms Appear Harsher When Put Into Print
- Different is not Necessarily Wrong

Phase-based Best Practices

- Integrated Risk Assurance Oversight Matrix
- Identify Risk-based Business Performance Assessments

Discovering Business Gold

- Foundational, Situational, Event-based, & Random Observations
- Random, Unannounced Inspections
- Assessment Calendars
- Executive Sponsorship
- Multidiscipline Teams
- Seek Local Participation for Context
- Independent Assessors
- *advocatus diaboli* – The Devil's Advocate
- Assess the Good, the Bad, and the Ugly
- Observation Announcement Timing
- Use of Standard Observation Forms
- Documented and Signed Observations
- Data Synthesis
- Identify Data Relationships
- The Use of Models
- Diverse Models
- Validate the Extremes
- Integrity Without Excuses
- Measure Against Excellence
- Define Issue Materiality
- Three Whys Deep
- Identify the Hidden Drivers, part 1
- Identify the Hidden Drivers, part 2
- Avoid Using Absolutes
- Who's on First?
- Don't Break the Mirror
- Show It Visually
- Separate Fact from Opinion
- Avoid Jargon
- Capture Improvement Opportunities within the Corrective Action Program

Phase-based Principles, Best Practices, and Warning Flags

- Training, Grading, and Quality Assessments

Phase-based Warning Flags

- Inwardly Focused Performance Assessments
- The Illusion of Accuracy
- Using Data as Information
- Absence of Evidence as Evidence of Absence
- Distinction Without a Difference
- Intellectually Empty Assertions
- Massaging the Message for the Boss
- The Normalcy Bias
- Crediting Good Intentions
- Effort Bias
- Conclusion Bias
- Content Without Context
- Distinction Without a Difference
- Identifying Mostly Strengths

Phase-based Principles

The Vertical Slice Approach

All company functions are constrained by limited resources. As such, it is impossible for an organization to self-assess every activity it performs. Therefore, assessments need to be executed in a way that identifies the significant improvement opportunities at the lowest possible cost. One such approach is to do a thorough end-to-end review of a few occurrences of high value process.

The vertical slice represents such an end-to-end process evaluation; covering all transactions and organizational transitions as a process is executed from initiation to planning, scheduling, execution, and final closure. Performing a detailed review of appropriately selected processes yields insights to the process bottlenecks, organization misalignments, supporting system inadequacies, and personnel skill gaps that once improved offer the organization a significant return on investment.

Selecting Processes for Vertical Slice Assessment

When using the vertical slice assessment method, it is important to select high value processes to be evaluated. These processes are not limited to those that yield high revenue generation for the company but can also include those representing a significant cost to execute. Criteria to consider when selecting processes for vertical slice assessment include but are not limited to:

- Cost of executing the end-to-end process

- Impact to bottom line revenues of the end-to-end process
- Risk associated with the end-to-end process and the cost incurred should an error be made
- Frequency of process execution and the aggregate cost of execution (e.g. process that is inexpensive to perform executed frequently may have a higher aggregated cost of execution than a process that is expensive to perform and is infrequently executed)
- Number of employees involved with execution of the process (the greater the number the more complex the process and the greater the likelihood improvement opportunities exist)
- Number of employees performing the process within a specified period of time
- Number and severity of issues arising during routine performance of the process

Performing an End-To-End Process Evaluation

End-to-end process evaluations are intended to be thorough; identifying process, technology, and execution shortfalls and their causes. While not all inclusive, the following is a sample list of items that should be looked at during an end-to-end process evaluation:

- Total time to execute the process
- Time to perform each activity
- Time to transition between one activity and another, particularly when the transition represents a hand-off between individuals or organizations
- Points in the process where backlogs exist
- Points in the process where individuals experience downtime because they are waiting for the preceding activity's completion

- Redundant data entry within a single system
- Instances where data is not transferred between software applications when multiple systems are used during process performance
- Manual data manipulation when such calculations can be performed by the supporting application
- Instances requiring authorization when such permission is provided by default
- Activities performed multiple times or by multiple individuals when such activities do not significantly reduce the risk of error
- Data checks performed by individuals that could be performed by a properly configured software application
- Transition points hindrances resulting from the manual transfer of data between systems, geographic and/or time separation of task performers, and inadequate communications mechanisms
- Process execution that is slower than allowed by regulation or policy
- Individuals who are over-qualified for assigned tasks / opportunities to assign tasks to less qualified, less expensive personnel
- Individuals who are performing tasks that could be delegated to personnel at lower level positions within the organization
- Activities performed by people that could be performed by software applications
- Process points where errors frequently occur
- Times in the day when process errors frequently occur
- Times relative to the organization's daily schedule that errors commonly occur

As with all assessments, the answers to these questions should be derived from direct process execution observations, record reviews (completed process forms, error reports, corrective action requests, root/apparent/direct cause analysis reports, etcetera), application data reviews, personnel interviews, and procedure reviews. The combination of facts derived from these studies is then used to formulate and validate improvement opportunity hypothesis.

The Horizontal Cut Approach

An organization's limited personnel resources necessitates that its business performance assessments be performed in the most efficient manner possible. While at times there may be the need for an in-depth end-to-end process review, at other times it will be appropriate to examine performance of a specific task or activities by numerous performers from across the organization. On these occasions, the horizontal cut assessment approach is most appropriate.

Selecting Activities for Horizontal Cut Assessment

Rather than focusing on a few occurrences of a sequence of activities as does the vertical slice, the horizontal cut focuses on the numerous performances of a single activity. Subsequently, those high value activities on which to focus the horizontal cut assessment should be determined by:

- Task or activity presenting a significant personnel, equipment, or other business risk
- Task or activity within a high value process (as determined by the vertical slice assessment method) that takes a relatively long time to perform
- Task or activity within a high value process having a relatively high error rate
- Task or activity within a high value process that is performed manually, particularly those for which there is no additional error prevention measure applied
- Task or activity within a low value process for which errors have resulted in a significant cost to correct

- Task or activity having an extremely high performance rate
- Task or activity having a modestly high performance rate and a relatively high number of users performing the task or activity

Performing a Cross-Organizational Activity Evaluation

The horizontal cut assessment approach examines one or a few tasks/activities performed by a multitude of people from across the organization. This assessment approach is particularly appropriate when a given activity is performed by a large number of individuals within the organization or when the activity is performed a relatively high frequency. Key activities performed during this type of assessment include:

- Evaluate of the task time performance data to identify above average, average, and below average performance; enabling ready identification of performance best practices and opportunities for improvement
- Examine task related data; often in spreadsheet format to allow for rapid review for consistency/outliers and errors
- Perform direct observation of a cross-organizational sample of activity performers to identify physical; environmental; tool; oversight; and program, process, and standards barriers to efficient successful performance
- Review past changes to the activity's performance (methods, procedures, tools, applications) to identify alterations that unintentionally hinder contemporary performance or were improperly implemented when declining performance is noted

Data gathered and examined should be further segmented by department or other work group to identify the differences in performance within the overall organization. Consideration should be given to the frequency of activity performance by department/work group members when comparing productivity and error rates.

Combination Assessment Approach

Something is not right... performance seems okay but the organization is not moving forward, not learning, not developing, as it should. The spark of innovation, the passionate drive to excel is gone from the leadership team and workforce. Sales may be stagnate or declining. Or perhaps asset experience one too many failures to be considered normal.

Whatever the circumstance, executives and managers often find it difficult to isolate the cause of stagnate or diminished performance to any reasonable degree. They recognize, however, the need to identify and eliminate the underlying, deep-rooted issues so to ensure continuity of operations and viability of their organization. With limited time, financial, and personnel resources, how can these hard to identify issues be surfaced and addressed?

Combination Assessments

Employing a combination of horizontal and vertical assessment approaches within a single evaluation enables problem isolation and deep insight gathering. While somewhat more resource intensive than a normal assessment, combination assessments increase the likelihood of problem identification over performance of one or a series of vertical assessments and greater insight gathering over performance of a single horizontal assessment.

Performing Combination Assessments

Combination assessments are performed in a manner that first isolates an issue and then performs a deep dive evaluation to identify its root causes.

Issue isolation begins with a series of increasingly deeper horizontal assessments, each more narrowly focused than the preceding evaluations. The series of horizontal assessments often include:

1. Review of organizational performance measures individually and in groups to identify performance issues (programmatic performance) or areas (work groups)

2. Review of underlying data reports providing greater insight into the specific drivers of reflected performance with a focus on identifying programs and work groups involved

3. Selected ad hoc data analytics to further isolate the programmatic or organizational areas involved

Once the series of horizontal reviews has isolated an issue to a particular program or work group, a vertical assessment should be performed to obtain insight to the underlying causes of the issue.

Combination Assessment Applicability

Combination assessments should be used in the following circumstances:

- Stagnate performance is exhibited broadly across the organization
- Stable performance improvement exhibited at rates less than that of the industry average
- Apparently random, unrelated asset failures at a rate that is somewhat higher than normal

- Appearance of a new, higher level of adverse condition performance (e.g. sustained higher rate of attrition over past periods)
- Executive/Manager gut feel or intuition of an issue but without a specific focus area

Yellow Sticky Analysis

Business performance assessments represent a second tier aggregation of organizational data, benchmarking references, and industry experience. As such, assessment team members are challenged to combine the often disparate data they collect in a way that allows them to draw meaningful conclusions upon which the organization can act to improve performance.

Not all organizations possess the financial, technological, and personal resources required to effectively employ complex analytical tools but all should have access to the wonderful product known as the yellow sticky. Using a yellow sticky analysis technique, assessment team members can aggregate data in high level categorical groupings that foster more the detailed analysis necessary to draw meaningful, actionable conclusions.

Performing a Yellow Sticky Analysis

Yellow sticky analysis organizes assessment collected data into high level functional and cross-functional categorical groupings that enable team members to readily identify patterns among what previously seemed to be unrelated data points in order to derive meaningful performance improvement conclusions. This method of data analysis is performed in the following manner:

Step 1: Document factual observations gleaned from the analysis of numeric data, activity observations, personal interviews, and individual surveys

Step 2: Transpose factual observations onto individual yellow sticky notes

Step 3: Based on the subject of the assessment, identify the functional performance areas which the final report will address. For example, if supply chain performance is being evaluated, functional areas may include procurement, inventory management, warehousing, returns, and warranties

Step 4: Label individual pieces of easel paper with the functional performance areas identified

Step 5: Assign each yellow sticky note to the functional area to which it is most related. Depending on the number of yellow sticky notes associated with each grouping, further subdivide these areas into subtopics. For example, inventory management may be further subdivided into safety stock, cycle stock, in-transits, reorder points, category management, segmentation rules, etcetera

Step 6: Further divide the yellow sticky notes associated with each functional and sub-functional area into groups related to people, process, and technology

Step 7: Analyze each yellow sticky note grouping (functional area in whole and people, process, and technology grouping within each functional area) for common performance trends

Step 8: Develop a beneficial practice or shortfall statement (as applicable) associated with each identified functional/sub-functional performance trend

Discovering Business Gold

Step 9: Review the people, process, and technology findings across each functional/sub-functional area to identify cross-functional performance trends broadly applicable to the organization

Step 10: Develop a beneficial practice or shortfall statement (as applicable) associated with each identified cross-functional performance trend

Note that one fact may be associated with multiple functional and/or sub-functional areas. In these instances, create duplicate yellow sticky notes for this fact and apply them to all of the appropriate functional and/or sub-functional areas. Once the yellow sticky analysis is completed, associate facts duplicated in this manner with the one beneficial practice/shortfall it most supports. Using each fact only once within the final report prevents the perception of undue use of any single item.

Final Thought...

In our experience, conclusions reached through a yellow sticky analysis are the most robust when all members of the assessment team participate in the exercise. This includes involvement by the members of the organization being assessed so to ensure the incorporation of local context.

Criticisms Appear Harsher When Put Into Print

Fact or fiction, anything formally documented assumes an air of legitimacy. Combine this implied legitimacy with the stark black and white of the printed words and any identified improvement opportunity can appear overly harsh and critical, especially to those responsible for the performance. Apparent aggressiveness within a assessment can result in resistance to the evaluation findings; often by those who stand to benefit the most and who must own the corrective actions.

Avoiding defensiveness while still conveying improvement opportunities and their importance is the challenge faced by all assessment leaders. While total resistance avoidance is not realistically achievable, following these few principles will help make assessment findings more palatable and accepted:

- Provide situational context
- Avoid the use of absolutes
- Back up assertions with at least three facts each
- Facts should be observable and quantitative whenever possible
- Provide validated, observable, and quantitative external benchmarks
- Discuss assessment facts with those being evaluated throughout the assessment process to afford them the opportunity to validate the facts on which conclusions will be based
- Present assessment findings in person; being available to provide additional commentary as requested

Principles one and two help the assessment read better by respecting the situation of those assessed. Principles three, four, and five ensure the assessment is credible and that those assessed can personally validate the facts. Principles six and seven ensure open dialogue affords the assessed an opportunity to offer fact validation and context and provides them the opportunity to express their opinions and conclusions for consideration.

Respect for those being assessed and credibility of the report, achieving these goals will help the report read less harshly or at least be more accepted.

Final Thought...

Business performance assessments are not effective unless the message delivered is heard and acted upon. However, assessors will sometimes encounter situations where unexpected or undesired evaluation findings result in management's summary rejection of the report in part or whole under all circumstances. When these situations occur, it is important to remember that the integrity of the assessors and the report are more important than finding acceptance. It is always better to fail on the side of the truth than to succeed by unduly softening or distorting known realities.

Different is not Necessarily Wrong

People naturally take pride and ownership of their work. This pride drives them to believe their approach is the right or, at least, the best method for performing the activity; often closing off any consideration of other methods.

Nothing could be further from the truth. There are certainly many ways to skin a cat and more than one executive has overseen his/her company's demise because of a failure to adopt others' better ways of conducting business.

This concept applies to the performance of assessments as well. All too often, assessors conclude that because an activity is not performed using their method that there exists a performance improvement opportunity. They fail to consider results achieved, resources consumed, waste generated, or any other quantifiable factor or circumstance that would support the different performance approach.

Assessors can avoid the 'different is wrong' by asking the following questions of the methods being evaluated:

- What results are being achieved as compared with the approach I would recommend?
- What resource inputs are required as compared with the approach I would recommend?
- Does the organization have access to the resources needed to implement my recommended method?
- What wastes are generated as compared with the approach I would recommend?

- Are their beneficial uses of the wastes generated as compared with those evolving from the approach I would recommend?
- Are there other more successful organizations using the method I would recommend?
- What might be the outcomes achieved if I implemented the method being evaluated in place of that which my organization is currently employing?

Different may be suboptimal or even wrong but there should be quantifiable evidence to substantiate that claim. Failure to make the quantifiable case suggests a preference that is neither right nor wrong, it is opinion.

Phase-based Best Practices

Integrated Risk Assurance Oversight Matrix

Maintaining compliance in today's highly regulated, rule-driven marketplace requires diligent oversight of the organization's core processes by the company's staff. This oversight takes many forms from internal audits, business performance assessments, management observations, and quality checkpoints embedded within the processes themselves.

These points of oversight, however, may individually fall short from providing fully effective compliance risk assurance. Therefore, deliberate action should be taken to marry these assurance activities into a single cohesive program.

The first step in establishing an integrated risk assurance oversight program is to identify those internal activities providing assessment coverage of the organization's core processes and programs. Such an assessment matrix relies on the clear identification of core organizational processes typically grouped by function or functional like organization accompanied by a listing of the various internal persons and groups providing deliberate, focused and routine assessment of the effectiveness of the program's implementation that necessarily includes compliance with government regulations and industry standards. The matrix is further enhanced when additional details of the oversight activities, such as evaluation frequency and specific areas of coverage, are covered. Figure 2, Core Process Risk Assurance Matrix provides an example of one such matrix.

Final Thought...

While an organization must rely on its own internal or directly contracted resources to provide effective oversight, such oversight activities benefit from the insights provided by governmental regulatory and industry evaluative activities. Therefore, truly best practice risk assurance matrices will also include those external bodies providing oversight to the various core organizational processes with equally detailed frequencies, focus areas, and other such information as is collected and documented for the internal assurance activities. By documenting the external organization oversight mechanisms, internal assessors are provided a clear line-of-sight to other relevant information sources when performing their evaluations. Likewise, business leaders receive a complete portfolio listing of oversight activities their organization will be subjected to.

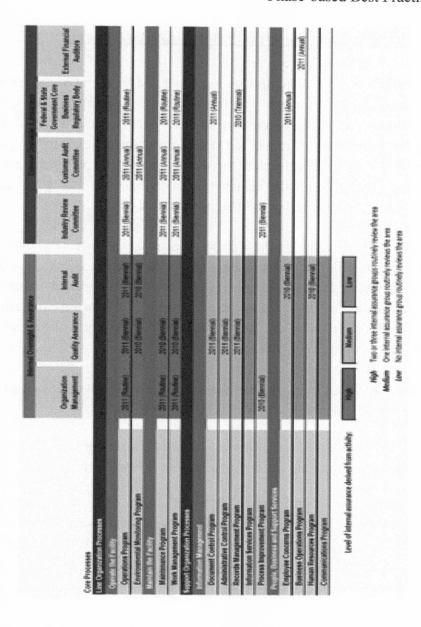

Figure 2: *Core Process Risk Assurance Matrix*

Identify Risk-based Business Performance Assessments

Organizations expend significant personnel and financial resources on well-performed business performance assessments and the implementation of follow-up performance improvement actions. To reap the appropriate return on their investment, executives and managers must carefully select the assessments to be performed such that they directly support achievement of organizational goals and values while mitigating its most significant risks.

Identifying high-value business performance assessments is an iterative process derived from the organization's risk assurance map. After development of the risk assurance map, including the incorporation of all internal and external oversight activities, the following evaluation should be performed (in the listed order) in order to identify the highest-value assessments to be performed:

1. Identify those performance areas assigned a high risk score for which no internal assessment is being performed.

2. Identify those performance areas related to organizational goals and values for which no internal assessment is being performed.

3. Identify those performance areas for which there are regulatory assessments but no corresponding internal assessment. Particular attention should be given to those areas for which the failure to comply with a regulation could have a moderate to significant adverse organizational impact.

4. Identify those high-risk, organizational goals and values performance areas for which one or a very few internal assessments are being performed and consider assessing these areas in the 'off years'.

Having identified a collection of high-value assessments, planners should organize these evaluations into a well-integrated business performance assessment calendar.

Final Thought...

Organizational risks and goals as well as regulatory requirements change over time. As such, risk assurance maps should be updated from time-to-time, often on an annual basis aligned with the updating of the organization's risk matrix. Once updated, a new map evaluation should be performed to ensure the highest-value business performance assessments continue to be pursued.

Foundational, Situational, Event-based, and Random Observations

While management observation programs serve many purposes, they primarily exist to drive achievement of the organization's goals in a manner consistent with its values. These formal, documented observations accomplish this by shaping and reinforcing personnel behaviors critical to supporting excellent operational performance. To provide adequate coverage, these observations should be performed on a recurring, situational, event, and random basis.

Proper observation timing ensures both managers and contributors remain faithful to the organization's operational performance guidelines during routine ongoing operations as well as high-risk evolutions. This timing includes:

- *Foundational Observations* – observations occurring at a given frequency within a defined time interval. These observations typically focus on those broad-based behaviors required during most, if not all, operations

- *Situational Observations* – observations targeted at specific high-risk activities to ensure risk mitigating behaviors are demonstrated during these critical times. These observations occur during the preparatory training for and performance of high-risk activities and not at any specific time interval

Another class of situational observation supports assessment and/or benchmarking activities. These observations are performed in advance of the assessment or benchmarking activity to provide additional, timely information in support of these activities

- ***Event-based Observations*** – observations performed after a significant performance expectation violation that sets a dangerous precedent or causes significantly adverse impacts to the organization. These observations are performed across a broad number of organizational groups, especially those performing similar operations to that group in which the violation occurred, so to identify the extent of condition of the undesired behavioral deviation and to broadly reinforce adherence to the proper management standards

- ***Random Observations*** – observations reinforcing desired behaviors performed at the discretion of the individual observer without any specific activity relationship or time constraint. Such random observations reinforce with employees the need to be ever vigilant to the adherence of workplace standards because their compliance may be monitored at any time

Well-constructed management observation programs define, schedule, and monitor performance of foundational, situational, and random of observations. (Event-based observations are added to the plan as needed and set to occur for such a time as management deems necessary to effectively reestablish and reinforce the desired behavior.) Managers responsible for the organization's operational programs in consultation with senior leaders who help identify the key risks to be monitored typically identify the specific observations to be performed on an annual basis. The resulting observation matrix is then broadly communicated to those leaders responsible for observation performance.

Random, Unannounced Inspections

It's perfectly natural and expected that individuals want to do a good job and be recognized for it or at a minimum want to do a good enough job to avoid what are to them undesired consequences. Subsequently, people look to what their superiors communicate as required job performance to gag the level and timing of their efforts.

Irrespective of the specific performance standard, routine performance measurement timing often drives undesired behaviors. This frequently overlooked performance driver is itself a performance standard, one that indicates the narrow time frame within which performance matters. Individuals tend to heighten their performance during this short measurement period when 'it really matters' and relax their efforts during other times. Random, unannounced inspections help overcome this performance decline phenomenon.

Random, unannounced inspections help keep an organization's members operating near peak performance on a continuous basis. To receive the greatest benefit from these inspections without overly stressing employees, consider the following principles when implementing a random inspection process:

1. Random, unannounced inspections are conducted within all organizational business units and workgroups

2. Inspections focus on activities and processes critical to mission performance

3. An unannounced inspection frequency should be established relative to the immediately preceding formal or random inspection

of that area. This frequency should allow enough time for the evaluated organization or individual to implement and realize results from corrective actions coming out of the preceding inspection but not be so long as to allow for a lax in performance

4. Organizations to be inspected are made aware of the unannounced inspections no earlier than reasonably needed to gather required records and schedule personnel interviews and observations without significantly impacting business operations

5. Unannounced inspections evaluate performance more broadly and deeply than the few performance measures covering the applicable activity or process

6. Random, unannounced inspections follow the same evaluation process as formal, scheduled inspections including data gathering and evaluation, briefings, reports, and follow-up actions

7. Inspection outcomes contribute to organizational and individual performance evaluations in a manner similar to that of scheduled inspections and routinely maintained performance measures

Final Thought...

Fundamentally, managers should expect individuals to perform such that they are not afraid to have the boss look at their work or know what they are doing at work. Those individuals adhering to this standard by doing their very best at work will always be *inspection ready*.

Assessment Calendars

Continuous performance improvement requires focus on both near-term operational priorities and long-term strategic capabilities and initiatives. In order to be optimally effective, performance assessments must be performed in a timely manner such that the subsequent recommended improvement activities can be implemented and affective prior to key operational events. Furthermore, the right organizational resources – *particularly personnel* – must be available to successfully conduct any assessment. By using assessment planning calendars, program coordinators gain the prerequisite insight to schedule assessments and resources far enough in advance to achieve these two imperatives.

Benefits of an Assessment Calendar

A well-planned assessment calendar provides numerous coordination and resourcing benefits to the business performance assessment program manager/group and operational business groups. Some of these include:

- Helps provide time to fully implement improvement recommendations before the occurrence of associated key events/activities
- Promotes coordination and availability of operational personnel to support assessment performance
  Reduces the business performance assessment program's impact on operations (because of resource leveling – see Developing an Assessment Calendar below)
- Reveals the subject need and timing for benchmarking information

- Enables identification of near and long-term business performance assessment program knowledge, skills, and experience needs, including the proactive acquisition of external consulting support when needed

Types of Assessments to be Scheduled

A robust continuous performance improvement program consists of several different types of assessments; monitoring core business risks, operational goals, and organizational values while also accounting for dynamic organizational, operational, and environmental changes. Annual business performance assessment calendars commonly include the following types of assessments:

- *Foundational Assessments* – assessments occurring at a given frequency within a defined time interval typically focused on core business risks, operational goals, and organizational values

- *Situational Assessments* – assessments targeted at specific high-risk activities to ensure risk mitigating behaviors and mechanisms are present during these critical times. These assessments include reviews of the integrated training, execution, and follow-up improvements associated with these events

- *Event-based Assessments* – assessments performed after a significant performance expectation violation that sets a dangerous precedent or causes significantly adverse impacts to the organization. The assessments scans a broad number of organizational groups, especially those performing similar operations to that group in which the violation occurred, so to identify the extent of condition of the undesired deviation and to broadly reinforce adherence to proper management standards. Note that the business performance assessment and corrective action programs should also be examined to determine why precursor deviations were not identified and corrective action taken prior to the event's occurrence

- **_Random Assessments_** – assessments reinforcing desired behaviors performed at the discretion of the business performance assessment program manager and/or senior organization leaders. Such random assessments reinforce with employees the need to be ever vigilant to the adherence of workplace standards because their compliance is monitored at all times

Developing an Assessment Calendar

Integrated assessment calendars combine the evaluation schedules of all of the organization's internal and external oversight groups. Individual assessments assigned to the calendar are optimally derived from a risk assurance map that aggregates and prioritizes these activities against the organization's primary risks, goals, and values. Once the assessment activities are identified, they are migrated to an annual assessment calendar by week. The assessment schedule is then optimized by performing the following:

1. Assessment activities are ordered in 'swim lanes' according to the functional workgroup, facility (bundled functional workgroups), and business unit (bundled facilities) being evaluated

2. External assessment activities are assigned to their respective weeks as scheduled by the external assessment organization

3. Internal assessment activities are assigned to a calendar week based on the following factors:

    a. Ahead of an associated event so to ensure enough time to implement identified corrective actions and realize their benefits

    b. Coordinated with major activities to be performed

    c. Aligned with other related assessments so to enable the synergizing of common activities and sharing of related cross-functional information

4. Internal assessment activity timing is adjusted to levelize the organization's overall internal and external assessment burden by:
   a. Functional Workgroup
   b. Facility
   c. Business Unit

Note that event-based and random assessments will not be scheduled. These will be performed on an as-needed basis.

Executive Sponsorship

There tends to exist a perception that companies are generally open to the identification and resolution of problems; that resources will be applied to solve issues if the gains expected can be shown to outweigh the costs. Reality is frequently different. Priority setting driven by limited resources and at times less visible agendas often precludes an organization from addressing small tactical issues and large global initiatives.

Members of the executive team are uniquely positioned to understand the organization's direction, see the competitive landscape, and make priority-based decisions regarding the deployment of the organization's limited resources. Therefore, executive sponsorship is critical to ensure that performance of a assessment will be well supported and its findings acted on.

Executive sponsors provide many invaluable resources to an assessment team. Namely, they offer:

- A span of control and command over organizational resources needed to perform the assessment and implement its recommendations
- An integrated view of the organization's performance and its external environment that will enhance the assessment's overall perspective and be used to appropriately prioritize the performance of the assessment and implementation of any subsequent recommendations in light of the organization's other commitments
- Influential relationships with other key executives, customers, and stakeholders which are critical in achieving buy-in for in successful implementation of assessment recommendations

In addition to their contribution to the assessment itself, executive sponsors frequently use their position to mentor and develop members of the assessment team. Team members benefit from the often deeper and more varied experience of their executive sponsor; learning how to more effectively interact with executives and senior managers, gaining a richer understanding of the complex interactions between the business environment in the organization and outside of it, and becoming skilled at communicating change broadly across the organization and to external stakeholders.

Multidiscipline Teams

Complex business processes often involve many of the functional business units within an organization. Regardless of the process specifics, it is unlikely a single individual will possess the broad range of knowledge and experience needed to fully understand the influences and impacts each functional contributor has on the process's overall outcomes. Therefore, when evaluating cross-functional programs, processes, and procedures it is critical that a multidiscipline assessment team be employed.

Multidiscipline teams help ensure the full range of needed knowledge and experience resources are brought to bear when evaluating a complex program, process, or procedure. Having enough knowledge and experience resources occurs when the team includes individuals that together possess the background necessary to recognize significant beneficial and adverse performance drivers. By extension, this implies that not all functional disciplines need be represented during every assessment. Additionally, as an assessment progresses, circumstances may arise requiring engagement of personnel possessing knowledge and experience not originally identified as needed for the evaluation.

Seek Local Participation for Context

Properly performed business performance assessments provide business leaders with deep insights as to what is working well and opportunities for improvement within a business function, area, or process. These insights become even more beneficial when the practices and results of top performers are used as a reference or benchmark for the evaluation. Best practices, however, are not always relevant to every situation or circumstance. Therefore, it is important to consider local context when evaluating performance against accepted best practices.

No one better understands the local performance context than those who work within it every day. These individuals know from experience what drivers, written and unwritten, cause the organization to function as it does. For this reason, assessment teams benefit most when receiving the local perspective from an objective, top performing member of the organization being assessed.

Important to the success of the assessment team, including the local content provider, is the clear definition of this individual's role. The context provider should not be assigned to the assessment team to defend his or her organization or to 'soften' the assessment team's findings and recommendations. A context provider's role is to provide:

- Perspective of the organization's performance over time
- Insight to the cultural and behavioral norms accepted within the organization, both written and unwritten
- Historical events driving implementation of policies, practices, and procedures

- Organizational circumstances and situations incompatible with the specific best practices being considered
- Guidance as to whom the team should interview and/or observe to gain additional insight; including making introductions to these individuals
- Direction as to how needed documents and information can be obtained
- Facility tours and access guidance/coordination

If the assessment is formally presented, the local context provider should attend so to be available to offer the stakeholders receiving the report any additional perspective they may desire.

Final Thoughts...

Participation on a business performance assessment team is a broadening experience; offering team members an opportunity to learn about the organization as well as interact with senior leaders. Therefore, the position of local context provider should be given to those rising stars who will use the opportunity to further their professional growth. Additionally, because the local context provider gains firsthand experience with the assessment process, these individuals are excellent candidates to serve on the assessment teams valuating other parts of the organization; yet another development opportunity for the rising star.

Independent Assessors

An individual's perception of circumstances and events is largely shaped by his/her knowledge and experience, beliefs, values, and biases. In the organizational setting, this perception is influenced by the organization's shared history, its culture, and the individual's relationships with seniors, peers, and subordinates. Additionally, event perception is often limited by the individual's finite, relevant knowledge and experience, as well as his/her employment impact concerns and desire for self-promotion. To be effective, a strategic analysis must be free of the impairments and limitations individuals within the organization have when assessing internal events and impactful external circumstances.

Independent assessors are often engaged by an organization in order to evaluate internal performance and external environmental conditions in a significantly more unbiased manner. Because these outsiders are free from the organization's vestiges, they tend to be able to provide executives and managers with a more accurate picture of performance, including hard-hitting and insightful opportunities for improvement. The independent assessor's perception of conditions, occurrences, and organizational factors gives him/her several advantages over internal evaluators including:

- Not biased by the organization's shared history and culture
- Less relationship driven or biased
- Typically possess knowledge and experience beyond that resident within the organization, in particular, those learned from interactions with other similar companies
- Significantly less employment impact risk for identifying organizational shortcomings

These factors also serve to enhance the independent assessor's credibility with executives and managers; increasing the likelihood that action will be taken based on the recommendations presented.

While independent assessors are often thought of as outside consultants hired by the organization to perform a particular evaluation, they may come from a variety of different sources including:

- Consultants
- Government inspectors
- Benchmarking partners and peer mentors from outside the organization
- Employees from other business units, departments, or crews

Regardless of the source of the independent assessor, it is important that these individuals be sufficiently removed from the organization so that they are not subject to the biases common to those within the group being evaluated.

advocatus diaboli – The Devil's Advocate

Shared experience, organizational pride, and/or conflict avoidance can diminish the criticality of data and conclusion assessment; leading to exaggerated optimism and resulting in an organizational pursuit of unrealistic goals. Inflated expectations may drive investment in projects well outside of the organization's risk tolerance. In today's aggressive marketplace and under intense shareholder scrutiny, missteps like these can be disastrous for a company and its executive team.

Employing a Devil's Advocate throughout the assessment and decision-making processes helps prevent the unintended consequences of group-think. As a contrarian, the Devil's Advocate deliberately assumes a position opposed to the consensus viewpoint. He or she actively seeks opportunities to discredit supporting information and challenge seemingly logical conclusions. By attacking the group's position, the Devil's Advocate demands a rigorous defense be presented by the evaluating group; ultimately strengthening the final decision.

The Devil's Advocate is itself a challenging position to fill. Some organizations have one or more individuals who naturally assume this role. For those not having a resident skeptic, the position of Devil's Advocate can be assigned on a rotational basis in order to *share the wealth*. In either case, the contrarian qualities of critical thinking and questioning attitude are worthy of development in all managers and executives.

Assess the Good, the Bad, and the Ugly

"Don't throw the baby out with the bath water."

Thomas Murner (1475 – 1537)
German satirist and poet
Author of *Appeal to Fools*

Many business professionals almost singularly focused on identifying and fixing 'the ugly' – shortcomings that result in their organization's most adverse outcomes. This focus is understandable as extremely poor performance can cause irreparable damage. The approach, however, omits critical examination of a range of organizational performance, 'the good' and 'the bad;' placing the organization at risk of achieving only suboptimal performance.

What is good, bad, and ugly performance?

The good, the bad, and the ugly represent a range of organizational performance. Performance not included by these three characterizations are those commonly expected behaviors driving neither exceptionally strong nor poor performance such as showing up to work on time.

- *The Good*: those deliberate behaviors resulting in highly positive business outcomes

- *The Bad*: traditions no longer yielding exceptional or even positive results that go protected because of an organizational unwillingness to change or even challenge these actions

- *The Ugly:* intentional and unintentional actions driving undesirable results that must be stopped so to prevent adverse outcome recurrence

Why evaluate positive outcomes?

Assessing positive outcomes often appears to be a waste of precious time… or is it? A lot can be learned from the study of positive outcomes including:

- Was the outcome the result of luck or deliberate action? We'll take luck but it cannot be counted upon. Deliberate actions can be repeated. These should be recognized, documented, and trained on so they can be repeated.
- Were the positive results achieved driven by your actions or the failed attempts of others? Sometimes it's not a matter of winning, it's that the other team loses.
- Can the good actions drive positive outcomes in other areas? If so, they should be broadly communicated and practiced.
- Who or what group contributed to the desired results? These individuals should be recognized and rewarded to promote continuation of the exhibited behaviors.

It is important to look for the good even when assessing the bad and the ugly so as to not eliminate the performance of desired behaviors when correcting the performance resulting in adverse outcomes.

What's wrong with the bad?

The bad can be deadly for an organization. When these '900 pound guerillas' go unchallenged, they stifle a business's growth; providing innovative competitors an opportunity to seize market share. Examples of such destruction include Compaq, Kmart, and Zenith.

StrategyDriven has long advocated the use of a 'Devil's Advocate.' We also recommend the employment of these principles when evaluating overall organizational performance. It is the expressed role of this individual to challenge the organization's sacred cows.

Long-term practices and commonly held beliefs to be challenged are characterized by:

- Activities receiving whispered decent but not open challenge
- Undocumented but measurable practices
- Approaches uncommon elsewhere within the organization's industry or general marketplace
- Drivers of outcomes that are seemingly incongruent with societal norms

Some sacred cows drive the organization's success. This good should be acknowledged. However, portions of these practices may be outdated so even the best practices might need adjustment.

Evaluating the ugly goes without saying...

Of course an evaluation program must assess adverse outcomes and underperformances. Recurrence of negative outcomes needs to be prevented and lagging performance improved if the organization is to achieve long-term success. High-risk programs, those that could result in ugly outcomes, should also be evaluated to minimize the chance of realizing undesirable events.

Observation Announcement Timing

Philosophically speaking, no one, including managers, should ever be afraid to have 'the boss' know or observe what he or she is doing. Being human, we naturally feel self-imposed pressure to perform well especially when we are being watched. Subsequently, management observations will always make the conscientious employee at least somewhat nervous. When then does a manager announce that he or she will be observing an individual's performance? In most cases, shortly before the observation begins.

Why not announce the intent to perform the observation well in advance?

Management observation programs seek to identify the actual performance practices of the workforce. Announcing the observation well in advance of its performance allows those being observed to study and practice for the observation, often artificially changing what would have otherwise been the employee's performance. While in some cases this results in artificially (and only momentarily) improved performance, at other times performance significantly declines as employees wrongly guess at what the manager wants to see and deviate from established practices. Additionally, some employees will unduly dwell on the fact that they are going to be observed; assuming the reason for the observation is prior poor performance and elevating their workplace stress at the detriment of productivity and performance quality.

When should the intent to perform a management observation be announced?

Management observations should be announced shortly before commencement of the activity to be observed (see Defining '*Shortly Before*' below). This allows the individual to be observed the opportunity to recover from the very natural surprise from the announcement without giving them an extended opportunity to become anxious or nervously dwell on the situation. Additionally, the observed won't have time to prepare themselves into a different performance state; providing the manager with first hand insight into actual workforce performance.

Defining 'Shortly Before'

Depending on the activity to be observed, announcing the observation 'shortly before' will reference different timeframes. The following general principles should be considered to determine when to announce a management observation:

1. Prior to the beginning of work; no mid-activity surprises

2. Typically no earlier than the beginning of the day or shift the observation is to be performed

3. 30-60 minutes before the typical activity preparation reviews, material gathering, tool selection, site preparation, etcetera begins while still adhering to Principle 2

    Note: Complex activities for which preparation occurs days or shifts in advance should have their observations announced at the

---

beginning of the day, shift, or 30-60 minutes before the start of the activity whichever comes later.

Note: the manager should consider observing the preparation activities too as these will yield additional invaluable insight into employee performance

4. At the beginning of the observation. This is a second announcement to remind the employee that he or she is now being observed

Use of Standard Observation Forms

In order to be fully effective, a management observation program must have credibility with those being observed and provide organizational performance improvement information. Credibility is established when those observed can expect both repeatable evaluations by one manager and consistent evaluations by different managers for a given job performance relative to established standards. Organizational performance improvement information is yielded when evaluation data from across the organization is aggregated; providing insights to the common patterns of desired and undesired employee behaviors.

Achievement of these four goals is most easily accomplished when standard data collection forms are used during the performance of management observations. Fundamentally, standard management observation forms are performance expectation checklists on which observation facts are recorded. These checklists drive consistency between observations because managers using them are provided with a preestablished list of items and standards against which the employee's performance is judged. This consistency coupled with documentation of observation facts enables easy retrieval and aggregation of like data that can then be counted, trended, and analyzed to establish a picture of organizational performance.

While not an all-inclusive list, effective management observations forms typically possess the following qualities:

- Expectations to be observed are consistent with documented and communicated performance standards

- Each expectation observable has a well-documented and communicated graded performance range. A space is provided to document the grade for each observation area

  (*detailed grading criteria is often captured in a separate management observation process document*)

- Area for documentation of an overall activity performance grade and grade justification comments
- Space is allowed for the observer to document the specific behaviors witnessed
- Header space is available to document the activity observed, name of the observer, name of the individual observed, and the start and end time and date of the observation
- Signature lines exist for the observer and observed accompanied by a date and time

  (*the observed individual signs to acknowledge receiving the observation feedback*)

- Unique observation forms exist for various job types or standards adherence observations
- Listing of observables are logically grouped such as:
  - By task: job preparation, job execution, job follow-up
  - By performance standards: use of personnel safety techniques, use of personnel safety equipment, execution of personnel safety procedures
- Easily accessible, often available at the locations where the relevant work will occur
- Portable, often printed on pocket-sized note cards up to a single 8½ by 11 sheet of paper
- Rigid, printed on heavy weight paper or accompanied by clipboards for ease of use in the field

Final Thoughts...

While management observation of actual job performance is most effective, these observations can be extended to the finished or in progress deliverables of the workforce. In these instances, standard management observation forms provide a performance checklist for items such as the completeness and quality of staff work or the state of a job site. Note that it is important these observations are followed up with feedback to the individual responsible for the work's performance. These 'non-activity' type observations must adhere to *all management observation conduct best practices* to be fully effective.

Well documented management observations serve a dual purpose. Not only are they used to identify organizational performance trends but they provide managers with documentation of observed employee performance that can be used during routine feedback and coaching sessions and annual/semi-annual performance appraisal development.

Documented and Signed Observations

Robustly implemented management observation programs offer many benefits to the organization and its managers. At their core, each of these benefits is derived from aggregation and analysis of the performance data gathered during the observations. Enabling required data synthesis necessitates the documentation of observed occurrences and conclusions. Desired behavior reinforcement and performance improvement, not to mention manager and observation program credibility, necessitate the employee be briefed on the observations made and conclusions drawn. As with all formally documented performance appraisal instruments, the documented observation should be signed by both the manager and employee.

I understand the need to document observation findings but is having the manager and observed employee sign the observation form really necessary?

Absolutely! These signatures are a very tangible demonstration of accountability on the part of the manager and employee. For the manager, his or her signature represents ownership for an accurate and impartial evaluation of the employee's performance and the sometimes difficult and uncomfortable communication of the performance assessment to the employee. The employee's signature acknowledges receipt of the performance appraisal. While the employee may disagree with some or all aspects of the evaluation, signed receipt makes him or her accountable for the feedback and therefore responsible for continuing the desired behaviors and correcting the performance shortfalls identified.

Discovering Business Gold

Data Synthesis

Evaluation control programs must be credible in order to add meaningful value to the organization. Credibility is built not only by the quality of the data collected but also by the method by which it is collected, how it is combined, and how it is interpreted to create useful information in support of decision-making.

Data synthesis or data combination should be performed in a manner that enhances the credibility of the conclusions drawn. This process is comprised of two important parts: data prioritization and data association.

Data Prioritization

Begin with the Most Credible Data - data having high accuracy or believability. Examples of data from high to low credibility include:

- What we see - observable, measurable
- What we read - what others observed, measured
- What we hear - what others tell us, opinions

Begin with Refined Data - data having human intelligence and analysis incorporated into the findings; often by individuals closer to or directly involved with the occurrence or possessing special skills and experience in data analysis. Examples of data from high to low refinement include:

- Root cause analysis
- Business performance assessment reports
- Apparent cause analysis

- Benchmarking comparison reports
- Management observation reports
- Organizational performance measures
- Condition reports, operating logs and records
- Surveys, opinion polls

Begin with the Most Significant Data - data gathered from impactful events; revealing true organizational values and common behaviors because people tend to return to their core convictions and primary habits during times of increased stress.

Begin with the Most Recent Data - data representing the way things are or what is rather than the way things were or what was. The time period representing recent data varies depending on the rate of change of the parameter of concern.

Data Association

Ensure Only Like Data is Combined - data having equivalent meaning, units, time frames, and absolute references can be relatable. Combining data not possessing these qualities may lead to logic errors when making decisions including:

- ***Bad Analogy***: claiming that two things are similar when they aren't
- ***Extended Analogy***: claiming that two things related to a third are therefore, by extension, related to each other
- ***Argument from Spurious Similarity***: suggesting two items sharing some similar characteristics is evidence of a relationship between them
- ***Equivocation***: asserting the existence of a relationship between multiple items by associating a word with more than one meaning

to each differently; one with one meaning, another with a second meaning, and so on

Ensure No Double Counting of Data - individual data points occurring more than once in a combined data set. This circumstance can occur when combining two or more refined data sources based on one or more common underlying facts and tends to result in over-stated conclusions.

Following these guidelines will enhance the accuracy and credibility of the information presented to decision-makers. Improved accuracy reduces decision risk while increased credibility enhances the confidence decision-makers have in their chosen direction. Thus, sound data synthesis, through proper data prioritization and association, enhances the organization's opportunity for success.

Identify Data Relationships

"Information is data that has been processed in such a way as to be meaningful to the person who receives it."

Answers.com

Quality information supports effective decision-making. Data by itself, however, is not information.

Organizations are frequently data rich and information poor. Without proper contextual interpretation, data remains as sets of discrete points and offers little value to the complex decision-making necessary for organizational success. Therefore it is necessary to identify data interrelationships and to consider these when interpreting the data so to produce accurate, useful information.

Robust data interpretation requires multidimensional interpretation based on the interrelationships with and dependencies on other data sets. While not all inclusive, the following list provides common data relationships that should be considered:

- Programmatic inputs, outputs, and relational dependencies
- Employee availability; including knowledge, skills, experiences, absenteeism, and engagement
- Employee performance
- Operational decisions; including those affecting internal and external factors impacting the data set/point, management's attention, etcetera
- Equipment availability and up-time

Discovering Business Gold

- Technological limitations and anomalies
- Financial resource availability
- External market (marketplace, societal, and regulatory) influencers
- Biases in data collection
- Completeness of data; including the use of substitutions, assumptions, proxies, and gaps

Experience should also be applied to the interpretation of data so to identify otherwise not readily apparent relationships, causes, contributors, and insights. Note that over-reliance on experience may unintentionally limit the consideration of and openness to new influencers.

Final Thought...

Data can be difficult to interpret. Just as it is important to employ multidimensional evaluation of data, multidisciplinary teams can further enhance data interpretation and greatly expand the amount and value of information yielded.

The Use of Models

In today's data rich world, it is often difficult to identify the meaningful patterns and relationships that yield information decision-makers need to set the direction of their organizations. Additionally, complex market environments create a multitude of data analysis options; preventing any one person from seeing every possibility. Deriving compelling information from this sea of data and presenting it in simplistic, understandable, and actionable manner thus becomes the challenge of every business analyst. Helping solve this dilemma is the business model.

The power of models is threefold. First, models harness the knowledge and experience of people internal and external to the organization; knowledge and experience that has been tried and tested under a multitude of circumstances. Second, models are easily updated, often automated, providing results in near real-time. Third, models present information in a simplified view that is commonly tailored to suggest a particular course of action.

Model Risks

As with any tool, there exist certain risks when using models. Applying the wrong model to a particular circumstance can provide information that drives inappropriate actions leading to disastrous results. Constructing an overly simplified picture risks omission of influential nuances that may subsequently challenge the realization of desired outcomes. Therefore, those using models and analyzing their results must fully understand the model's and data's limitations as well as the situations for which the model is valid. Results, especially extremes, should always be validated for reasonableness and applicability.

Final Thought...

Applicable models will not be available for every situation or circumstance. During these times, multidiscipline assessment teams help bring to bear an increased level of knowledge and experience as well as raising the amount of data that can be evaluated. These teams can be further enhanced by the participation of peers from outside the organization.

Diverse Models

Solutions addressing today's multifaceted business challenges and opportunities can be extremely difficult to recognize; the ever increasing pace of change within the business environment further complicating this problem. In order to successfully deal with this challenge, decision-makers need the support of people and tools to help them distill large quantities of data, recognize important business trends, discount temporary fads, and translate their findings into meaningful organizational activities. Because no one analysis perspective will adequately account for all of the important nuances associated with a complex problem, multidiscipline teams and diverse tools should be employed to establish a complete picture of organizational performance and environmental conditions. Use of a diverse set of models during the strategic analysis process helps create this needed picture.

As discussed in *The Use of Models*, organizational leaders benefit significantly by using models to help them sift through the mountains of available data and to recognize the meaningful patterns and relationships that yield the information needed to make timely decisions. Yet as is the case with all measuring instruments, an individual model can only evaluate one or a few characteristics of organizational performance or environmental conditions. Therefore, multiple models, each targeted at a different aspect of performance, should be used to paint a complete performance picture from which decision-makers gain the insight and understanding needed to make quality decisions.

Final Thought...

Use of diverse models to analyze organizational performance and environmental conditions is akin to using an assortment of organizational performance measures and multidiscipline teams. This practice provides varying perspectives on the same situation, leveraging a broader data, knowledge, and experience base, and subsequently more fully characterizing existing circumstances and future opportunities which in-turn helps decision-makers identify the appropriate course of action.

Validate the Extremes

Performance studies of today's intricate, technology-driven organizations and the fast paced business environments in which they operate yield unprecedented amounts of data. Analysts often employ complex algorithms and visual models to synthesize and process this data into meaningful information that organization leaders use to formulate their company's direction.

Mathematical modeling, however, can sometimes provide analysts with misleading information. Because they seek to characterize performance while accounting for a broad range of unique circumstances, models and other forms of statistical analysis often assume a normal results distribution and subsequently rely on average values. This reliance on averages, in turn, may mute an impactful occurrence at the extreme of the performance range. Thus, it becomes important for analysts to validate performance extremes.

An Example

Consider the following example. A customer survey is performed to assess the quality of a company's product. Twenty-five customers are asked to rate the product's quality during the first three months of ownership on a scale of 1 to 5, 1 being unacceptable and 5 being excellent. Figure 3, Survey Results Sample Data, graphically illustrates the feedback received.

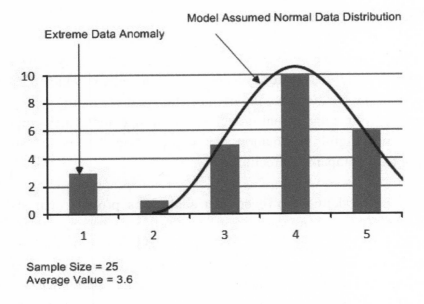

Figure 3: *Survey Results Sample Data*

Because the product is considered to be a price-leader within its category, a minimum initial quality rating of 3.5 was desired. The actual quality rating received, reported as an average, was 3.6; satisfying this goal. However, examination of the extremes using a simple bar chart reveals that twenty percent of all survey participants gave the product a 1 or unacceptable rating. This significant number of low quality ratings warrants further investigation by analysts and, most likely, the attention of and corrective action by company leaders.

Final Thoughts...

Validating the extremes occurs not only at the edges of the data range, but also includes validation of background assumptions and unexpected results.

It is equally important to remember that validating the extremes is not limited to simply identifying conditions that warrant further investigation. Validating this data implies that analysts will probe deeper to identify why these anomalies exist so to provide leaders with the information they need to make actionable decisions; even if the decision is to take no action.

Validation of the extremes is also a best practice defense against the adage of "if it sounds too good to be true, it probably is." Regardless of the circumstances, analysts should review their model and statistic-driven findings for:

- Omissions and anomalies
- Unpredictable results as the end of data ranges
- Reasonableness and consistency with known realities

<u>Integrity Without Excuses</u>

For any assessment to be effective, it must be done with an open, honest assessment of the facts. Organizations acting with *integrity without excuses* seek to identify and eliminate instances where fact-based assessment conclusions are diluted by unrelated factors or opinion-based influences. This mitigation often seeks to justify action perceived as desirable when the fact-based evidence would suggest another course. Justification is frequently based on business factors that are not specifically value related or biases lacking a relevant performance basis.

Compliance Does Not Equal Excellence

- Local and federal regulations establish minimum performance standards to protect the organization and the public against unacceptable, adverse consequences. These regulations not established for the purpose of creating business value and represent a cost of doing business. Therefore, value-based business decisions between competing alternatives should not be made solely on the basis of regulatory requirements. While an organization must meet the minimum regulatory requirements, additional actions may yield significant business value; making such efforts worthy of pursuit.

- Under similar circumstances, organizations acting with *integrity without excuses* assess alternatives differently than those tending to take a minimalist approach. Organizations acting with integrity will meet the regulatory requirements and claim the job 'well done' because 'we meet all of the requirements and don't need to do any more.' Organizations acting with *integrity without excuses* will meet the regulatory requirements and challenge themselves to identify and pursue activities beyond those defined by the regulations that add substantial value to the business. These organizations don't equate excellence with compliance but rather equate excellence with the maximization of the business's value.

It Can Happen Here

- Organizations acting on bias also tend to forgo potential business opportunities. In these cases, assessment conclusions are discounted because of a belief the conclusion could not be true of or apply to the organization. Such biases are often rooted in the organization's performance history; the past successes and failures experienced with various products, services, business units, individuals or the business environment.

- Organizations acting with *integrity without excuses* seek to eliminate decision bias in several ways. While decision-making balances facts and experience, members of these organizations validate the relevance of their experience to the circumstances of the decision to be made. Additionally, they seek to understand and apply the circumstantially similar experiences of others. Finally, they employ techniques, such as the devil's advocate, to challenge their decisions from different perspectives in order to eliminate potential organizational bias.

It can be extremely difficult for an organization to always act with *integrity without excuses*. Reinforcement of this behavior must come from the top to prevent subordinates from diluting 'the message' to one they believe will be acceptable to the boss. However, only when a strategic analysis is performed with *integrity without excuses* and the complete message delivered can decision-makers select the most value adding course for their organization.

Discovering Business Gold

Measure Against Excellence

In this hyper-competitive business world there are no points for second place. Companies not achieving excellence in key performance areas as defined by their chosen market often find themselves driven to irrelevancy by competitors and in danger of going out of business. Subsequently, organization leaders must know how their company performs against standards of excellence in the key areas to be able to make the investment decisions necessary to remain competitive.

Measuring performance against standards of excellence provides a clearly defined, uniformly applied reference point and does not mean the company should seek to achieve excellence in all areas. Achieving performance excellence in the several critical competitive areas as defined by the organization's industry and market positioning is necessary. For all other performance areas, a measurement against excellence provides executives and managers with a reference to what is achievable; enabling them to more fully understand the possibilities for improvement and more likely to assess the merit of these opportunities as a way to advance the business.

Defining Performance Excellence

Identifying quantitative measures of performance excellence can be a difficult process. The following principles and sources are recommended to ensure appropriate performance references are defined.

Principles

- Identify the key areas for which performance references will be sought based on the company's industry and market strategy
- Seek performance references from companies within multiple industries; identifying the organization's industry performance reference separately
- Use multiple companies to determine the excellent performance standard; leveraging the performance citations of reputable evaluators to focus the assessment process
- Avoid using averages; instead identifying truly excellent performance
- Refresh each performance reference periodically; based on the area's criticality to the business's success

Sources

- Trade associations and industry organizations (including their publications), such as the Nuclear Energy Institute and the Electric Power Research Institute
- Functional area membership organizations and professional organizations (including their publications), such as the Project Management Institute and Society for Human Resource Management
- Publically available data, such as company statements and government reports
- Management consultants
- Onsite benchmarking of other companies

Presenting the Performance Excellence Reference

Organizational performance in key areas should be broadly and routinely communicated. These communications will take several forms including performance metrics and reports, as well as assessment and benchmarking reports. And while the leadership's established performance criteria should always be prominently displayed, reference to the standard of excellence should also be included.

Presenting organizational performance against the single marketplace standard of excellence provides only a partial picture of performance. As performance data is collected from multiple benchmark organizations, an attempt should be made to show performance in a quartile framework. The performance of the company's various business units, as well as, that of its direct competitors can also be plotted in this quartile framework to present a complete overview of the competitive landscape.

Define Issue Materiality

Business performance assessments seek to identify *meaningful* improvement opportunities for an organization, typically in the areas of safety, performance reliability, and operational efficiency. Meaningful or *material* opportunities are those representing a performance improvement that satisfies a regulatory requirement, exceeds the organization's financial return on investment threshold, and/or provides a not easily replicable advantage over competitors. As such, assessors should evaluate potential performance improvement opportunities for their materiality; focusing on those offering the organization meaningful gains.

Determining Materiality

Materiality represents the threshold at which a performance improvement opportunity is significant enough to warrant the investment of time and resources required for its implementation. Consequently, materiality is relative to the size and circumstances of the individual organization being assessed. Some questions to consider when evaluating an identified performance improvement opportunity's materiality include:

- Is the improvement required by statute or regulation?
- Did the deficiency result in a regulatory required reportable condition?
- Does the improvement mitigate or eliminate an unsafe personnel or equipment condition? Has the deficiency resulted in a significant production, customer, and/or financial loss (often defined as 10 percent or more)

- Is the shortfall chronically impacting ongoing operations, current or future initiatives, and/or reported business results?
- Will the operational efficiency and/or reliability gain meet or exceed the organization's return on investment threshold when considering the cost of implementing the improvements?
- Can the improvement provide the organization with a not easily replicable competitive advantage that will meet or exceed the organization's market share goals?
- Does the improvement reinforce the organization's values?

While material findings should meet one or more of the above conditions, these findings should possess all of the following characteristics:

- Relevance: Material findings will influence management's decisions
- Reliability: Omission or misstatement of a material finding will impair management's ability to make good decisions
- Completeness: Material findings must be complete in order to present an accurate and fair view of the conditions to be improved or resolved

Final Thought...

Focusing on material findings is not intended to suggest that all observed facts should not be documented. On the contrary, documenting and assessing all observed facts in aggregate is necessary to identify material findings. Additionally, these documented observation facts can contribute to other evaluation activities including causal analysis and individual performance reviews.

Assessors should also define the materiality of the corrective actions they recommend. All corrective actions have an implementation cost and just as an organization's business initiatives should clear a return on investment threshold. Performing corrective actions for the sake of being viewed as 'taking action' is damaging to an organization as it robs from it the scarce resources that would otherwise be applied to more valuable activities.

Three Whys Deep

Executives, managers, and individual contributors familiar with the day-to-day workings of their organizations undoubtedly know or have contrived the reason for 'why things are the way they are.' Beyond this understanding, sometimes at an unconscious level, these individuals will perceive one or more drivers to these organization shaping whys. What remains unseen and unthought-of of are the tertiary and lower level drivers to why the business performs as it does. It is here that truly useful insight can be gained; insight enabling the foundational changes needed to alter the organization's direction and propel it to the next level.

To be of real value, assessments must get to tertiary and lower drivers; otherwise they are nothing more than simple collections of already known data. Assessors should therefore strive to ask three whys deep before drawing their final conclusions on organizational performance.

How to Get to the Third Why

Getting to the third why and its valuable insight can be challenging, after all, these drivers are largely outside of the organization's collective conscious. Therefore, the following method is offered as a means of third level driver identification.

Step 1: Identify and Document the Strength or Problem

Variability increases the further away from the source of organizational strength or challenge assessors probe. Therefore, it is critically important to precisely and concisely identify the strength or problem statement first. This statement should be documented and discussed by the assessment team to ensure unity of understanding.

Step 2: *Brainstorm Possible Level 1 Causes of the Performance Strength or Problem*

Performance drivers not considered by the assessment team, particularly at Level 1, may prevent the team from identifying the one insight that leads to breakthrough growth. Therefore, it is important at this stage to consider all possible performance drivers.

The most effective means of ensuring all potential performance drivers are considered is to consolidate the assessment team's collective experience in a performance driver identification brainstorming session. The outcome, the list of potential performance drivers, should be documented and communicated with the entire assessment team to ensure a common understanding.

Step 3: *Validate the Level 1 Performance Drivers*

Once a list of potential Level 1 performance drivers has been created, it will be important to identify which drivers play an active role in organizational performance. Only those impactful performance drivers will be considered in Step 4.

It is important to remember that not all identified potential Level 1 performance drivers will actually exist within the organization. Additionally, some drivers may exist but have little or no influence on organization behavior and so can be disregarded. Finally, validation of the relevance of the potential performance drivers will typically require some combination of document reviews, personnel interviews, and

Discovering Business Gold

in-field observations along with the subsequent data analysis and calculation.

Step 4: Brainstorm Possible Level 2 Causes of the Performance Strength or Problem

Like Step 2, it is important to leverage the collective experience of the assessment team in identifying potential causes of Level 1 drivers. As before, these potential drivers should be documented and socialized with the entire assessment team to ensure a common understanding.

Step 5: Validate the Level 2 Performance Drivers

Assessors should follow the approach described for Step3. Note that at this point, the reasons for organizational behavior are becoming more vague to both leaders and staff members. At this point, the diverse experience of outsiders, internal and external, become invaluable in 'seeing' past organizational predispositions and to the existence of performance drivers; particularly undesired drivers and those conflicting with the organization's values or self-image.

Step 6: Brainstorm Possible Level 3 Causes of Performance Strength or Problem

and

Step 7: Validate the Level 3 Performance Drivers

These steps are a repeat of Steps 4 and 5 respectively. Insights of organization outsiders become increasingly important now as conclusions drawn should be well outside of the organization's conscious. Whenever possible, driver validation should be supported by quantitative or a significant amount of collaborating qualitative evidence. If not already being done, assessors should routinely brief stakeholders to ensure ongoing buy-in for their conclusions.

Step 8: Conclusion Documentation and Communication

As with all assessments, the conclusions reached should be well documented and communicated to key stakeholders. Documentation should include enough detail that later readers of the assessment will not only understand the conclusion reached but will be able to logically follow the evidentiary reasoning for it. Communication should motivate those who can preserve good or improve on poor performance to do so.

Identify the Hidden Drivers, part 1

Organizational alignment to common goals suggests executive, manager, and employee motivation is largely driven by its strategic plan. However, there are likely some additional, hidden performance drivers unintentionally created by the organization's processes or embedded as an integral component of the organizations' history and culture.

When performing an organizational assessment, it is important to seek out and identify these hidden performance drivers and then to evaluate their alignment with the organization's overarching purpose. Likewise, it is important to understand where misalignments exist and whether or not they are resulting in behaviors detrimental to the achievement of the mission.

Hidden drivers are characterized as such because they are not the highly publicized measures of performance or operating philosophies commonly known by all members of the organization and often by stakeholders, shareholders, and the general public. Instead, hidden drivers often go unrecognized; uniquely influencing the individuals or small groups to whom the policy, procedure, or history applies.

Hidden drivers can be in both documented and undocumented form. Examples of documented drivers include: performance incentive program measures, performance incentive program time horizons, policies, procedures, and individual and work group performance measures. Undocumented influencers typically represent organizational culture and biases, including: complacency resulting from unevaluated, repetitive, and long-standing successes; an organizational tendency to shoot the messenger, and preferential treatment given or deferment of decisions to particular business units or individuals perceived as being important.

Hidden drivers are not necessarily detrimental to the organization's performance. It is important, however, that they be understood and assessed to ensure business planning and execution efforts are not diminished or undermined by these influencers of behavior.

Identify the Hidden Drivers, part 2

Simply put, people tend to behave in the manner for which they receive reinforcement. There often exists both documented and undocumented performance drivers that exert unintended pressure on individuals to act in ways counter to achieving the organization's mission goals. As a continuation of *Identify the Hidden Drivers*, part 1, this discussion expounds on several common hidden performance drivers and how they may adversely impact mission achievement.

Documented Drivers

- *Compensation and Incentive Plans*: By design, compensation and incentive plans reward individuals for specific behaviors. If the behaviors specified and rewarded are not aligned to the organization's goals, it is likely the individual will behave in a manner that diminishes mission achievement. The impact of misaligned compensation and incentive rewards is more significant at higher levels of the organization because of the greater influence and span of control these individuals possess.

- *Incentive Plan Time Frames*: In the case of executive incentives, payouts often occur at some future time in order to promote increased accountability for sustained organizational performance. However, these time frames may limit the duration of projects executives will endorse. The elevated risk associated with long-term projects represents a near-term risk to the executive incentive payout in order to realize a long-range gain for which the executive is not incentivized.

- *Workgroup Performance Measures*: Performance measures provide periodic, public reinforcement; driving individuals to behave in a manner that results in a positive measurement outcome, like compensation and incentive plans, if workgroup performance measures are not aligned with higher level and mission goals they will tend to drive behavior in a manner that diminishes mission achievement.

- *Policies, Procedures, and Standards*: People also behave in the manner which they are specifically directed, such as by policies, procedures, and standards. On occasion, these documents become misaligned with the organization's goals through a series of revisions in response to various events. When this occurs, performance unintentionally deviates from that which most directly supports mission accomplishment.

Undocumented Drivers

Undocumented Reasons for the Organization's Founding: Beyond the organization's mission statement, the reason for the organization's creation is usually understood and acted upon by the Board of Directors and/or a small select group of the senior leadership team. Rooted in the organization's history, this undocumented purpose guides decision-making at the top of the organization even when apparently counter to the stated mission. When this occurs, not only is the mission's achievement diminished by the direction set but there exists a risk of creating conflicting priorities for managers and individual contributors further limiting personnel effectiveness.

- *Organizational Legacy*: Organizations with a history rich in tradition and heroes may attempt to live up to or remain faithful to the legacy. Holding on to these past methodologies and philosophies may reduce the organization's efficiency in achieving its goals in today's rapidly changing, technologically driven marketplace.

- *Success Driven Complacency*: Organizations experiencing long periods of continuous success may over time question the need to seek improvements or change; believing that they represent the industry benchmark or standard. Today's highly competitive marketplace often leaves those who rest on their laurels struggling to remain viable.

- *Personal Relationships* **(or the lack thereof):** People tend to identify and form relationships with those they perceive are like themselves. This may result in the endorsement of the actions and recommendations of one individual over another for relationship reasons rather than as a result of an objective assessment. On occasion, the relationship-based selection will result in the lower value option being pursued.

- *Defer to Perceived Important Groups or Individuals*: Whether real or not, some groups and/or individuals are often perceived as being critically important to the organization. Abdication of decision-making to these individuals, especially on topics outside of their area of responsibility or knowledge and experience base, can result missed opportunities or increased adverse impacts.

- *Personal Agendas*: Hidden personal agendas often seek to enhance one's prestige and influence or protect one's position and expand one's span of control regardless of the overall organizational impact. Ego-driven power struggles of this nature can irreparably damage an organization and often result in missed opportunities because of the roadblocks erected by those who don't stand to significantly benefit from taking the action.

- *Unspoken Values*: Valuing certain behaviors or personnel characteristics may personally benefit a majority of organization members. Subsequently, these behaviors and personnel characteristics become part of the corporate value system even if these values are socially unacceptable and counter to optimal mission achievement.

Remember, hidden drivers are not necessarily detrimental to the organization's performance. It is important, however, that they are understood and assessed to ensure business planning and execution efforts are not diminished or undermined by these influencers of behavior.

Avoid Using Absolutes

Evaluators performing business performance assessments often find themselves awash in data suggesting their company's performance significant lags that of competitors and top industry performers. Evidence suggesting the need to improve may be so plentiful that the self-assessors come to believe immediate reforms must be made if to only ensure the continued viability of their organization.

All too often, the performance improvement focus of an assessment drives assessors to lose a degree of perspective regarding what their organization does right; even for those things for which they are recognized as an industry leader. Lacking a balanced perspective on their organization's performance, evaluators fall prey to the notion that no process, product, or person is adequate to the task and that everything and everyone needs to dramatically improve. Translated into the business performance assessment report itself, this overly negative perspective may result in the assessment team advocating the proverbial 'throwing out the baby with the bathwater.'

One easily employed method of reducing the likelihood of overstating the organization's performance improvement needs is to, at a minimum, challenge and often to avoid the use of absolute terms. Such terms typically point directly to overstated positions warranting further consideration. Absolute terms to listen for during routine team communications and oral presentations as well as in written notes, memos, and reports include:

- All, every, everyone, everything
- None, no one, nothing

- Always, forever, have to
- Never, under no circumstances

Final Thoughts...

There may be occasions where a assessment team finds no readily available evidence that corporate performance need to improve in one or more areas. The history of business reveals, however, that many significant advances came from the improvement or replacement of industry leading practices. Subsequently, the avoidance of absolutes is equally important, if not as often applicable, to the characterization of strong performance.

In some rare cases, the use of absolute statements is warranted and necessary. However, it is important that instances are recognized, validated, and deliberately and conservatively made so as to not diminish the credibility of the overall assessment findings.

Show It Visually

"A picture is worth a thousand words."

Fred R. Barnard

Individuals at all levels of an organization are under increasing pressure to do more and more in less time. Concurrently, they are bombarded with rapidly growing amounts of data that must be synthesized and processes into usable information and applied to their everyday decisions and actions. Consequently, methods of presenting information in a more rapidly digestible fashion greatly benefits the receiver and increases the likelihood that the conveyance will be recognized, understood, and acted upon.

In many respects, a visual image is worth a thousand words. Properly structured, graphic representations can depict large amounts of individual data points, convey relationships between data points, reveal trends in collected data, and draw comparisons between data sets. This information is concisely conveyed to the reader within a limited amount of document space and requires little assessment effort.

Types of Visual Representations

There are three primary types of visual representations; each serving to effectively convey information under a differing circumstance. Below are general definitions and use guidelines for each.

- **Graphs:** diagrams representing one or more data sets, including the interrelationships between individual data points or sets, trends, and comparisons. Typically used to convey numeric data

- ***Pictures***: images of a person, object, or scene. Often used to reveal visual characteristics of the imaged subject

- ***Illustrations***: drawn image of a person, object, or scene whereby numeric data is merged with the imaged subject's characteristics in order to convey compound information. Frequently used for enhanced communication that would otherwise require both graphs and pictures to convey

Information to Include with Visuals

As communicative as visuals are, brief statements of purpose and conclusion should accompany them. These one or two sentence statements all but eliminate the need for readers to assess the data's meaning; further enhancing the rate of information assimilation.

Developers should identify how their visual will be used. For those occasions when specific information is needed, data labels should be added to the visual to eliminate/reduce time spent acquiring this data from source documents.

Final Thought...

Using visuals is almost always appropriate. However, there are times when tabular data or textual discussions should also be provided. Situations where additional discrete data and/or context should be provided include those times where the reader must understand this data or when the data will be used to perform a task or make a decision. Visuals typically lead the detailed data so to provide a conceptual overview preparing readers for what follows.

Separate Fact from Opinion

Business Performance Assessment findings drive organizational actions. Consequently, a great deal of care must be taken when deciding what to include within a business performance assessment report. Findings based on logically derived conclusions founded on observable, quantifiable facts provide leaders with insightful information on how to improve performance. Findings built on opinion-based conclusions or founded primarily on individual experience frequently lack the vigorous underpinnings necessary to ensure a performance improvement opportunity. Thus, these suggestion-type findings should be excluded from formal business performance assessment reports.

Assessment team members bring with them invaluable experiences related to how the business operates, how the business could operate, and how other businesses operate to achieve desired results. These experiences, however, are limited to the "individual's field of view" and unlikely to include all critical aspects contributing to a given performance result. Consequently, conclusions reached primarily based on subjective experience may not actually afford the organization an opportunity to improve when examined more closely and tested with relevant operational data. Because many executives and managers feel bound to act on all assessment findings, inclusion of opinion-based conclusions without proper vetting may result in the inappropriate diversion of precious resources.

Eliminating Subjective or Opinion-Based Findings

In order to minimize the risk of opinion-based findings being included in business performance assessment reports, deliberate structuring of individual findings and report development should be practiced. In general, this involves:

- Documenting of three to five facts supporting each conclusion
- Validating the observation and quantification of each supporting fact by assessment team members and managers whose organization is being assessed
- Deriving and documenting of the conclusion drawn from a logical interpretation of the listed facts
- Vetting each finding by the assessment team, including employment of a Devil's Advocate
- Involving managers from the organization being assessed in the finding vetting process

Final Thought...

Subjective and opinion-based improvement recommendations founded primarily on personal experience are important for leaders to consider. These recommendations are appropriately brought to leadership's attention via the organization's business proposal or informal 'suggestion box' programs and should be accompanied by quantitative factual support to the maximum extent possible.

Avoid Jargon

Not everyone within an organization is a Harvard MBA graduate with a decade or more of business experience. Business performance assessors using highly technical terms as a way to impress others with their business acumen will often find that they confuse the very people they are trying to communicate with, namely, the organization's workforce.

In order for an assessment report to foster a high degree of organizational acceptance, it must possess a clear, concise focus and be translatable to the day-to-day actions of every member of the workforce. To achieve this, assessors should write the assessment report in a language familiar to everyone within the organization; incorporating words, phrases, and colloquialisms traditionally used by the workforce. An assessment report written in the organization's language will speak to and ultimately be embraced by its implementers.

Who's On First?

Clarity of communication is a critical component of all business transactions. Without understanding, we are prone to execute instructions in a manner different than that desired. So how then, can we as communicators ensure our message is clear and understood by those receiving it?

For communications to be clear, they must possess several key qualities, one of which is common language. Common language is more than a specific language; it also includes a common frame of reference. People from different locations often use words and phrases the meaning of which is not broadly understood. And even among individuals sharing a like understanding of this slang, an off-normal word association can inhibit understanding.

One of the best illustrations of two people speaking one language, English, but not understanding each other because of a lack of common reference is Abbot and Costello's *"Who's On First?"* routine first performed in the early 1930's.

Recognizing Common Language Challenges

Preventing communication misunderstandings will eliminate the often costly need for rework and renegotiation in addition to the damage done to relationships. Several activities that help identify when a common language challenge is likely to exist:

- Identifying the language and fluency level of audience members
- Learning the regional living differences of audience members

Discovering Business Gold

- Listening for requests for clarification or restatement
- Looking for the appearance of inquisitive or confused facial expressions
- Checking for alignment between audience member responses and information communicated

Minimizing Common Language Challenges

In addition to recognizing common language challenges, communicators can proactively minimize the occurrence of these misunderstandings by:

- Communicating in the language of the audience or employ an interpreter to do so
- Eliminating the use of colloquialisms from communications
- Checking for understanding of key messages and action requests
- Using visuals to augment verbal communications, particularly for complex or abstract concepts

Don't Break the Mirror

Feedback mechanisms serve as a reflection of an organization, business unit, department, or individual's performance. At times, these mirrors reveal exceptional performance; in other cases, good or satisfactory performance; and in some instances poor or unacceptable performance. Too often, the individual or group holding the mirror, whether a performance metric, an internal business performance assessment, or a third party audit, is blamed for the performance indicated. Regardless of who provides the performance report, this person or group should not be attacked for identifying instances of success or failure.

Organization leaders who 'shoot the messenger' create a chilling workplace environment that communicates to all employees the value of not reporting those performances or issues management may deem to be undesirable. Such behavior drives a wedge between leaders and their employees resulting in executives and managers becoming increasingly uninformed of the organization's needs and opportunities. The 'shoot the messenger' behavior takes its form through several practices, all of which should be avoided:

- Personal attacks levied against the individual(s) making the report, with or without the person being present
- Open reprisals against the employee(s), including reassignment, demotions, and terminations
- Documented and undocumented reprisals against the employee during feedback sessions, performance reviews, pay raises, and promotion boards
- Silent mistreatment of the messenger, including the withholding of feedback, job assistance, and future assignments; particularly those hindering the employee's development and advancement

Discovering Business Gold

- Silent dismissal and inaction toward resolving the presented findings

Final Thoughts...

The 'don't break the mirror' practice does not exclude providing constructive feedback to the presenter focused on helping this individual better communicate results in the future. Additionally, constructive challenge should be made to the findings themselves when underlying facts are in error.

The underlying premise of the 'don't break the mirror' practice is that leaders own the performance of their organization and need to take responsibility for that performance. They should hold themselves accountable for both the good and bad outcomes achieved and not attempt to avoid accountability by erroneously blaming the individuals(s) identifying credible issues.

Remember, leaders cannot delegate accountability.

Capture Improvement Opportunities within the Corrective Action Program

Self-critical business performance assessments yield multiple opportunities for performance improvement; yet their benefits often go unrealized because assessment recommendations are not acted upon. To ensure the organization profits from each assessment, it is necessary to programmatically pursue the recommended performance improvement actions*. The structured approach employed should drive accountability for implementing the improvement activities balanced with the organization's other priorities.

Effective corrective action programs capture the organization's identified performance improvement opportunities regardless of source, prioritize these opportunities in aggregate including the assignment of due dates, designate a responsible individual and apportion resources to implement the activities associated with each opportunity, and monitor activity progress to a timely completion. Consequently, the corrective action program is the process best suited for documenting and tracking the implementation of assessment recommendations so to ensure their benefit is appropriately realized.

Numerous benefits result from capturing assessment identified improvement actions within the corrective action program including:

- Identify issue/opportunity significance consistent with all submitted issues/opportunities/suggestions
- Establish action priority in aggregate with all other organization activities
- Assign and reinforce accountability for issue resolution

- Allocate resources to perform corrective actions consistent with the issue's priority relative to other activities and within the organization's limited resource capabilities
- Trace corrective and performance improvement actions to their identifying source
- Report on the status of performance improvement actions and associated results achieved for both individual assessments and the overall program
- Evaluate business performance assessment program effectiveness at driving performance improvement through the monitoring of action status and results achieved
- Analyze assessment findings over time in order to identify broader-based issues more deeply rooted in the organization's culture and/or programs that would otherwise go unobserved if such a broad-based analysis was not possible
- Perform causal analysis for issues associated with regulatory non-compliance and significant performance deficiencies that go beyond the scope of the business performance assessment program

---

* In this context, performance improvement actions refer to those activities needed to resolve a performance deficiency, mitigate an identified risk, enhance already satisfactory performance, or capitalize on an emerging opportunity.

Training, Grading, and Quality Assessments

Management observations profoundly influence the behaviors of those observed. Done well, this tool positively reinforces desired behaviors. Performed poorly, this tool will undermine the management team's credibility and fosters cynicism towards managers and their performance standards requirements. Therefore, it is critical that those performing these observations do so in a consistent, high quality manner.

Shaping manager and supervisor behaviors is no different than doing so for individual contributors. Leader behaviors must be observed and constructive feedback provided to reinforce desired action. In the case of management observations, this can be achieved through observation performance training, grading, and quality assessments.

Observation training ensures new managers and supervisors understand the organization's performance standards and can acceptably execute a management observation. This training should consist of the individual study of organizational performance standards and management observation program execution guidelines followed by an observation performance demonstration and concluded with a written, oral, and observation performance evaluation. Foundational management observation performance competency is established once the examination is passed.

Grading observations helps reinforce the ongoing quality standards set for management observations. Established criteria provide benchmarks against which each observation is assessed. The final grade is often used as a weighting factor against the observation's quota count to further reinforce quality standards.

Overall health of the management observation program should be periodically assessed to ensure effectiveness; observation quality being a key component of such assessments. Direct observation of management observation performance should be included as a part of this assessment to further evaluate observation execution quality and feedback. The results of the management observation assessment should be shared with all managers and supervisors in the spirit of helping them improve their own performance.

Note: The names of the managers and supervisors observed should be withheld from the business performance assessment report.

Final Thought...

For the individual contributor, the management observation program is a primary indicator of management's commitment to established performance standards. Any fault in observation performance will be viewed as acceptance and even endorsement of below standards performance. If not fully prepared and capable of performing the highest quality observation, then no observation should be performed at all.

Phase-based Warning Flags

Inwardly Focused Performance Assessments

Often practiced, it can be highly misleading to base the organization's performance standards relative only to internally identified best practice methods and characteristics. While at times the organization's performance does represent the highest standard, it is more likely that individual activities are performed more effectively and efficiently by other organizations, particularly those seeking to improve performance in an effort to compete with perceived industry leaders. Top performers recognize this trap and augment their internal search for effective performance with an outward examination of other relevant businesses.

Organizations that are too inwardly focused tend to lose sight of the business environment and often find aggressive, innovative competitors capturing ever increasing portions of the market. While not all inclusive, the four lists below, *Process-Based Warning Flags*, *Process Execution Warning Flags - Behaviors*, *Potential, Observable Results*, and *Potential Causes*, are designed to help organization leaders to recognize whether their organization is too internally focused when establishing standards of performance. Only after a problem is recognized and its causes identified can the needed actions be taken to move the organization toward improved performance.

Process-Based Warning Flags

- Business performance assessment processes do not require simultaneous examination of external benchmarks against which internal performance is compared

- Business performance assessment processes do not require the participation of team members from outside the organization or business unit being evaluated
- Business environment monitoring mechanisms do not include close examination of individual and process performance characteristics
- Lack or infrequent execution of external benchmarking

Process Execution Warning Flags - Behaviors

- Executives and managers do not promote the benchmarking and comparison of organizational processes and results to those of other businesses
- Resistance to performance comparisons on the basis that 'our organization is unique'
- Frequent executive or managerial rebukes to recommended changes based on external benchmarks
- Shoot the messenger' admonishment is given to assessment team leads and members when identifying performance shortfalls relative to that of other organizations
- Resistance to performance comparisons, particularly via a benchmarking, based on the perception that the activity's cost (time and expense) would not be justified by its benefit

Potential, Observable Results

- Business performance assessment reports lack comparisons to the performance of other organizations
- Costs of like products and/or services are consistently higher than those of competing organizations
- Declining or smaller profit margins as compared to similar businesses
- Loss of market share

Potential Causes

- Lack of or low organizational accountability
- Fear of job loss if benchmarking reveals more inefficient methods for performing business operations
- General discomfort with challenging the status quo, resistance to change
- An organizational culture that resists change on the basis of 'it was not invented here' and/or 'that is not the way we do things here'

The Illusion of Accuracy

"Measure with a micrometer, mark with a crayon, and cut with a chainsaw."

Author Unknown

Evaluation and control programs provide executives and managers with the critical information they need to make effective business decisions. However, an equally critical component of the decision-making process is the understanding that no data-set is a perfect reflection of reality. Therefore, it is important for business leaders to recognize the potential inaccuracies associated with their data in order to fully assess the risks these flaws pose to the achievement of desired outcomes.

The purpose of every evaluation and control program is to accurately represent the business conditions being monitored. Because of assumptions, averages, and/or approximations applied by evaluation processes and measurement systems, reality can never be perfectly represented. Leaders having an errant understanding of data accuracy will either over or underestimate the risk associated with decision options. Therefore, it is important for decision-makers to understand the accuracy of the data presented to them. Only with this information can the risks associated with each decision option be properly assessed and the decision-maker afforded the opportunity to select the best solution alternative.

The illusion of accuracy created by an evaluation method or measurement mechanism is a result of either the measurement process itself or the way in which the process is executed. While not all inclusive, the four lists below, *Process-Based Warning Flags*, *Process Execution Warning Flags - Behaviors*, *Potential, Observable Results*, and *Potential Causes*, are designed to help organization leaders recognize whether their evaluation processes and measurement systems unduly create the appearance of accuracy where less, little, or none exists. Only after a problem is recognized and its causes identified can the needed action be taken to move the organization toward improved performance.

Process-Based Warning Flags

- Analytical processes don't reinforce the application of mathematical principles for the use of decimals
- Documents are not screened for either the use of absolute terms and/or non-observable adjectives
- Procedures direct measurement beyond the limitations of prescribed measurement equipment, either out of range or less than one-half measurement increment
- Lack of independent information verification through the use of alternate measurement devices

Process Execution Warning Flags - Behaviors

- Conclusions stated as facts
- Assignment of emotional labels

- Lack of leadership challenge to the use of absolution terms or excessive numeric accuracy

Potential, Observable Results

- Distorted perception of actual circumstances Division between team members; often leading to deadlocks and infighting
- Faulted decisions, either overly conservative or aggressive
- Excessive use of decimal places
- Use of absolutes, such as all, none, always, and never

Potential Causes

- Undue desire for the feeling of security provided by having 'hard' data
- Misunderstanding or lack of knowledge and/or experience in the application of sound mathematic principles
- Lack of relevant situational experience resulting in excessive data focus
- Inability to relate past experience with current circumstances

Using Data as Information

Too often, individuals align themselves with a particular statistic or data point as though it infallibly supported their position. In these instances, raw data is assigned meaning absent context from the surrounding environment and possibly in spite of flaws and biases in its collection. While the assignment of meaning to a particular data point may serve one's immediate purpose, it often leads to erroneous conclusions and may result in undesirable outcomes.

For data to be of value in decision-making or driving behaviors, it needs to be properly interpreted both in context of other supporting and contradicting data sets and placed in context with other quantitative and qualitative environmental factors. Only when data is combined with other associated factors does it truly become information that can be appropriately used.

"Say you were standing with one foot in the oven and one foot in an ice bucket. According to the percentage people, you should be perfectly comfortable."

Bobby Bragan

Example errors in assigning meaning to a single or few raw data points include:

- Drawing conclusions from survey results without considering both the question asked and responder demographics

- Identifying trends based on the data from one performance indicator without the context of influencing operational factors and counter-balancing indicators
- Relying on averages particularly when derived from or highly influenced by extreme data points
- Making time-based performance evaluations without considering when data is counted, particularly near transition events such as shift turnovers, days, months, quarters, years, etcetera
- Committing logic fallacies when interpreting a single or limited number of data points
- Presenting data as possessing unsubstantiated accuracy often the results of manipulations using spreadsheets and scientific calculators

Representing an individual data point or statistic frequently leads to erroneous conclusions and poor decisions. Business leaders and professions must exhibit a skeptical, questioning attitude when presented with conclusions and recommendations so as to not fall into this trap. While not all inclusive, the four lists below, *Process-Based Warning Flags*, *Process Execution Warning Flags – Behaviors*, *Potential, Observable Results*, and *Potential Causes*, are designed to help organization leaders and individual contributors recognize whether they adequately process and challenge received data to ensure it has been properly contextualized. Only after a problem is recognized and its causes identified can the needed action be taken to move the organization toward improved performance.

Process-Based Warning Flags

- Data analysis processes do not provide guidance for data synthesis
- Data evaluation processes do not require the use of multiple inputs

- Data analysis processes do not engage local staff for contextualization
- Data evaluation processes do not engage multidiscipline teams for data interpretation

Process Execution Warning Flags – Behaviors

- Executives, managers, and/or individual contributors accept data and conclusions presented to them without question
- Organization members exhibit a lack of a questioning attitude when observing circumstances that differ with presented data, statistics, and/or conclusions
- Employees at all levels of the organization stop searching for other, particularly contrary information, once a data point or statistic is found that confirms their desired conclusion
- Executives, managers, and/or individual contributors frequently omit or cannot cite references for data or statistics supporting their conclusions

Potential, Observable Results

- Frequent number of events causing diminished productivity, higher costs, and elevated attrition for which precursor indicators existed but in retrospect had little visibility
- Organization becomes 'blindsided' by circumstances assumed not to exist or unconsidered during the decision-making process
- High or increasing decision failure rate

Potential Causes

- Executives, managers, and/or individual contributors feel it would be insulting to a presenter to challenge their conclusions

- Organization members erroneously trust data, statistics, and conclusions because of the individual presenting it (the corollary of the *ad hominem* logic error)
- Organizational leaders foster a workplace environment that does not challenge others, particularly seniors and peers
- Organization members rely on questionable sources of data or statistics to support their conclusions
- Employees are not trained on the proper qualification, verification, validation, of data sources

Final Thoughts...

Leaders should demand information, not data, during the decision-making process. Such a demand comes in the form of questions asked to challenge and explore the presented meaning behind the data offered and should address the data relationships and quality. It is not so important for a leader to have all of the answers but rather to ask the right questions challenging the conclusions presented.

Robust data interpretation requires multidimensional interpretation of the data based on its interrelationships with other data sets. Experience should also be applied to the interpretation of data so to identify otherwise not readily apparent relationships, causes, contributors, and insights.

Absence of Evidence of Absence

When examining organizational performance, assessors too often fall into the trap of concluding that the absence of adverse outcomes indicates a lack of underlying performance issues. This is an evidential fallacy. Many organizational shortfalls exist without causing consequential outcomes for reasons of redundant barrier prevention, lack of recognition, or simply blind dumb luck. The lack of a noticeable consequence does not necessarily equate to an absence of an issue; it simply means that the problem itself, up until the point of examination, has not manifested itself in a substantial outcome.

Drawing conclusions based on an absence of evidence is fundamentally a logic fallacy. Such errors often appear to be reasonable, common sense deductions and can therefore be difficult to prevent. While each logic fallacy has its own drivers, the four lists below, *Process-Based Warning Flags*, *Process Execution Warning Flags – Behaviors*, *Potential, Observable Results*, and *Potential Causes* provide executives and managers with some of the signs that evidential fallacy errors are impacting their organization's evaluations.

Process-Based Warning Flags

- Lack of an actual or designated contrarian, a devil's advocate
- Lack of or insufficiently defined evaluation methodologies
- Little or no logical reasoning training provided to executives, managers, and qualified assessors

Discovering Business Gold

Process Execution Warning Flags – Behaviors

- Over reliance on experience and intuition during assessments
- Willingness to accept conclusions without quantifiable evidence and robust data analytics
- Acceptance of a conclusion without significant challenge, including instances of group think

Potential, Observable Results

- Occurrence of significant, acute incidents often resulting in personnel injury, major equipment damage, and/or significant financial loss
- Unexpected accidents of significant consequence
- After-the-fact causal analysis commonly reveal numerous observable precursors that went unnoticed or unaddressed

Potential Causes

- Misapplication of logical reasoning often the result of a lack of logic application training and/or experience
- Organizational bias that favors the conclusion drawn
- Intellectual laziness
- Excessive time pressure, sometimes caused by a lack of resources, applied to the completion of evaluations

If the absence of evidence is not enough to substantiate the absence of a problem, then how can these illusive issues be identified?

Consider the following approach. If a problem were to exist, what might be the causes and contributors of that problem?

Assessors not finding evidence that a problem exists should pose the question of what factors might result in the yet to be manifest issue. Such artifacts can be found in procedures, standards documents, performance metrics, and management and workforce behaviors. In answering this question, assessors should consider the experiences of other internal and external organizations. In fact, learning from the operating experiences of others and challenging whether latent organizational issues exist before they are manifest can help a company to avoid negative outcomes.

The Positive Outcome Corollary

Just as a lack of negative results does not prove the absence of a problem, the existence of positive outcomes does not necessarily indicate the benefits of decisions, actions, and/or behaviors. Assessors need to carefully examine the circumstances of the outcome to identify where strong correlations exist between drivers and results. Simply citing positive achievements as an indicator of good performance is usually misguided and can serve to mask issues that can later result in significantly negative outcomes. In these instances, assessors must resist the overwhelming feeling of enchantment with positive results that leads them to too quickly concluding that a set of decisions, actions, or behaviors resulted in a desired outcome.

Distinction Without a Difference

"Six to one, half-a-dozen to another."

Author Unknown

While two or more things may be truly the same, people may attempt to characterize them as being different; drawing attention to characteristics or features that are either exactly or materially the same. These individuals seek to draw a distinction between the subject items where no difference exists.

Asserting that a distinction exists without a true difference places the decision maker and his/her organization at risk. These mischaracterizations of factual conditions distort the foundation upon which conclusions are draw and actions taken. As such, this logic error must be avoided.

While not all inclusive, the four lists below, *Process-Based Warning Flags*, *Process Execution Warning Flags – Behaviors*, *Potential, Observable Results*, and *Potential Causes*, provide insight to instances where decision makers make distinctions without a difference; unduly enhancing or diminishing a particular conclusion. Only after a problem is recognized and its causes identified can the needed actions be taken to move the organization toward improved performance.

Process-Based Warning Flags

- Decision making process does not require outcome quantification prior to option development

- Decision making process does not include rigorous fact documentation and characterization tools and/or methods
- Decision making process does not include a Devil's Advocate to challenge group think and logic errors

Process Execution Warning Flags – Behaviors

- Decision makers draw conclusions and then seek support for those conclusions
- Decision makers obsessively focus on immaterial factual quantities or qualities
- Decision makers narrowly focus on minute factual details
- Decision makers quickly dismiss opposing or challenging opinions

Potential, Observable Results

- Unnecessary or prolonged conflict between individuals
- Decision failure resulting in sub-optimal results, missed opportunities, significant expense, equipment damage, and personnel injury

Potential Causes

- Decision maker bias for or against the compared item
- Decision maker is generally an optimist or pessimist

- Decision maker inflated/misguided perception of the materiality of a quantity or quality
- Decision maker commits other logic errors when characterizing facts or conclusions leading to the errant perception of differences

Final Thought...

There are some instances where drawing a distinction without a difference has beneficial outcomes. These often occur in a motivational setting such as when a coach encourages his/her team not to beat the opponent but to dominate them. In both instances, the coach _is_ encouraging his/her team to win – no difference – but a distinction is drawn to inspire and motivate the team.

Intellectually Empty Assertions

Intellectually empty assertions represent logical laziness or deceit on the part of the individual(s) drawing these conclusions. Those making intellectually empty assertions do so without supporting facts, in contradiction of factual evidence, by incongruently combining two or more facts, through misapplication of real-world experiences or events, and/or commission of a logic error. Such assertions are not presented as opinion, but are instead forcefully put forth as representing either unchallengeable facts or as the only logical conclusion one could draw from the complete set of facts. There is nothing logical about intellectually empty assertions. Rather, these assertions tend to be made by individuals based on their personal biases, goals, or opinions and may drive disastrous outcomes if acted upon.

Intellectually empty assertions are particularly dangerous when used to make decisions or to influence the decision-making of others. Conclusions drawn from intellectually empty assertions tend to be irrational and emotional if not outright wrong. Consequently, severe adverse outcomes can result from this intellectual laziness or deceit.

Why Intellectually Empty Assertions Are Accepted

Individuals are influenced by intellectually empty assertions for a number of seemingly plausible reasons. Below are a few common mechanisms that induce individuals to accept intellectually empty assertions:

Reputation Boosters: Individuals succeed at influencing others with intellectual empty assertions through the use of one or more of the

Discovering Business Gold

following reputation boosters promoting their unsupported point of view:

- Personal stature and/or charisma
- Position and/or title
- Academic credentials, whether actually earned or honorary
- Direct and indirect association with others possessing some degree of the aforementioned reputation markers

Intellectual Laziness: Individuals who themselves are intellectually lazy or deceitful tend to accept the assertions of others possessing one or more of the aforementioned reputation boosters without themselves validating the underlying support for the assertions and forming their own rational, well-founded conclusions.

Need Fulfillment: Individuals having a strong emotional, financial, or other need fulfilled by the intellectually empty assertion may accept the assertion in order to satisfy their need.

Warning Flags Associated with Intellectually Empty Assertions

Intellectually empty assertions undermine sound decision-making. As leaders, it is our responsibility to ensure inputs to and conclusions from the decision-making process are logically constructed from verifiable facts, relevant experience, and sound judgment.   While not all inclusive, the four lists below, *Process-Based Warning Flags*, *Process Execution Warning Flags – Behaviors*, *Potential, Observable Results*, and *Potential Causes*, are designed to help organization leaders recognize and avoid intellectually lazy or deceitful decision-making. Only after a problem is recognized and its causes identified can the needed action be taken to move the organization toward improved performance.

Process-Based Warning Flags

- Data gathering guidelines do not ensure the reputation and credibility data sources
- Inputs to the decision-making process are not required to be qualified, verified, and validated
- Underlying decision facts and/or assumptions are not documented
- Decision-making process does not require the application of the Devil's Advocate
- Decision-making process does not provide for those resources necessary to reasonably alleviate time pressure
- Decision-making process does not adequately identify and recues those potentially having a conflict of interest with the decision to be made

Process Execution Warning Flags – Behaviors

- Decision-makers overly rely on 'gut instinct' and 'feel' to make decisions
- Underlying decision facts and/or assumptions are not presented or demanded
- Validity of underlying decision facts and/or assumptions are based on reputation boosters rather than on the merit of the facts/assumptions themselves
- Decision-makers and contributors judge information based on its source rather than its validity
- Decision-makers and contributors argue that they do not have the time to further validate underlying decision facts and/or assumptions

- Decision-makers and contributors overtly align underlying facts, assumptions, and conclusions with the perceived needs of the organization and/or members of the decision-making team
- Information supporting a foregone or desired conclusion is not challenged
- Information refuting a foregone or desired conclusion is not considered and/or its validity discounted

Potential, Observable Results

- Outcomes achieved are contrary to those expected, typically failing to yield few if any of the desired results
- Outcomes favor those making and possibly those accepting the intellectually empty assertions over others subjected to the decision's impacts
- Decision-makers blame other people and circumstances for the failure of their decisions to yield the predicted outcomes

Potential Causes

- Individuals making and/or accepting the intellectually empty assertions seek to further a personal bias, goal, and/or agenda
- Individuals making and/or accepting the intellectually empty assertions feel time pressure to reach a conclusion
- Individuals making and/or accepting the intellectually empty assertions lack the training necessary to recognize this decision-making shortfall
- Individuals accepting the intellectually empty assertions feel superior, peer, and/or subordinate pressure to do so

Massaging the Message for the Boss

Constructively critical business performance assessments often present executives and managers with a difficult to accept performance message. While intended to improve overall organizational performance, leaders may take these assessments as an affront to their authority or condemnation of their performance and some leaders may even retaliate against assessors. Additionally, lead assessors and team members seeking to gain the approval of those executives and managers who may positively influence their careers might themselves be overly concerned about the evaluation's messaging.

Lead assessors and team members frequently respond to leadership's adverse reaction or their personal ambitions by softening the tone of their business performance assessment reports. In extreme cases, they may even alter the report's perspective in order to please management. Such action greatly diminishes the assessment's value; robbing the organization of opportunities to improve. While not all inclusive, the four lists below, *Process-Based Warning Flags*, *Process Execution Warning Flags – Behaviors*, *Potential*, *Observable Results*, and *Potential Causes*, provide insight as to whether business performance assessment reports are being erroneously adjusted to accommodate personnel desires rather than reflecting actual performance. Only after a problem is recognized and its causes identified can the needed actions be taken to move the organization toward improved performance.

Process-Based Warning Flags

- Business performance assessment process does not ensure significant independence of the assessment team, particularly the lead assessor, from those executives and managers whose area of responsibility is being evaluated
- Executive sponsors can be those whose area of responsibility is being assessed
- Business performance assessment guidelines allow management to alter the final report's wording irrespective of the evaluation team's input
- Assessment guidelines allow for nondescript phraseology
- Assessment procedures drive qualitative over quantitative analysis
- No mechanism is in place to protect assessors from retaliatory action
- No mechanism exists to allow assessment team members to provide feedback on the evaluation process and final report, particularly anonymous feedback

Process Execution Warning Flags – Behaviors

- Lead assessors and team members omit information that may, in their perception, make their superiors look bad
- Lead assessors and team members promote the performance of those superiors who participate in their performance evaluations and promotion decisions
  Executives and senior managers silently mistreat assessment team members, including the withholding of feedback, job assistance, and future assignments; particularly those hindering the employee's development and advancement

- Executives and senior managers levy personal attacks against the individual(s) making the report, with or without the person being present, when the assessment findings are less than flattering
- Executives and senior managers commit open reprisals against the assessment participants, including poor performance ratings, withholding pay raises and promotions, reassignment, demotions, and terminations

Potential, Observable Results

- Business performance assessment findings are typically 'happy and glad'
- Business performance assessments result in only incremental improvements leading to slow/stalled performance improvement
- Organizational performance falls behind that of competitors

Potential Causes

- Insecure leaders demand positive performance reports for their area of responsibility
- Executives and managers do not understand or appreciate the tremendous value of an effective business performance assessment program
    - Executives and managers are more concerned about their individual success than that of the organization
- Lead assessors and team members are more concerned about their individual success than that of the organization
- Lead assessors and team members prioritize pleasing the boss over improving the organization
- Lead assessors and team members believe that making the boss look good will help advance their career

The Normalcy Bias

"It can't happen here..."

Sinclair Lewis (1885 – 1951)
American Novelist and Playwright
Winner of the Nobel Prize in Literature (1930)

...but what if it could?

Failing to adequately prepare for adverse events places an organization at significant risk. Indeed, such shortcomings have contributed to the fall of nations, demise of companies, and severe injury and death of countless people. Yet despite all of the evidence, many organizations today remain unprepared to deal with catastrophic events.

While it is impossible, if not impractical, to prepare for every eventuality, leaders sometimes ignore seemingly obvious risks. These individuals often suffer from a normalcy bias, a belief that because an adverse event has not occurred or affected them, that the event will not occur. This bias leads to the underestimation of both the probability and impact of an event resulting in a lack of preparation for the event.

Leaders afflicted by a normalcy bias may leave their organizations extremely vulnerable to catastrophic events. Furthermore, this denial may hinder event response if the situation   arises.   While not all inclusive, the four lists below, *Process-Based Warning Flags*, *Process Execution Warning Flags – Behaviors, Potential, Observable Results*, and *Potential Causes*, are designed to help executives and managers recognize misalignments between their organization's risk level and oversight coverage. Only after a problem is recognized and its causes identified can the needed action be taken to move the organization toward improved performance.

Process-Based Warning Flags

- Lack of or immature risk management program
- Long risk assessment / reassessment interval
- Lack of assessment follow-up procedures for identified risks / issues
- Lack of directives, policies, and procedures driving contingency planning particularly for high-risk decisions and infrequently performed tests and evolutions
- Lack of or immature operating experience program
- Lack of or minimal insurance coverage

Process Execution Warning Flags – Behaviors

- Inadequate Board of Directors and Senior Leadership Team oversight
- Emotions-based dismissal of risk evidence
- Discounting of external events and operating experience
- Dismissal of the need to perform contingency planning
- Non-compliance with written procedures

Potential, Observable Results

- Personnel injury and death
- Severe asset damage
- Catastrophic environmental harm

Discovering Business Gold

Note: These observable results often occur as lower impact events that increase in both number and severity over time until a catastrophic event occurs.

Potential Causes

- Misunderstanding of risk management principles and practices
- Logic errors in risk analysis
- Leadership bias towards / focus on internal experience
- Inwardly focused organization culture
- Excessively high risk tolerance

Final Thought...

A normalcy bias can be hard to recognize. Two intelligent people (or groups) can reasonably reach different risk conclusions based on the same data. Thus, what would be a *Black Swan*[1] event for one person may not be to another. For this reason, *StrategyDriven* recommends organizations prepare to flexibly and scalably respond to catastrophic events.

---

1. Black Swan events are unpredictable, catastrophic, and retrospectively believed to have been fully predictable. This definition is derived from Nassim Nicholas Taleb's book, *The Black Swan*.

Crediting Good Intentions

"The road to ruin is paved with good intentions."

German Proverb

Communicating assessment conclusions can be a difficult task, particularly in the case of improvement opportunities being presented to those directly managing or performing the function. Delivering the message is all the more difficult if those receiving it are organizationally senior to the assessment lead or are influential favorites of the organization's leaders. In these cases, assessment leaders seeking a tactful way of communicating the 'bad news' often fall into the trap of crediting the good intentions and/or self-identification of the issue by those responsible in order to put a positive spin on an otherwise negative message. Doing so, however, avoids the real issues at hand and can rob the organization of the opportunity to realize substantive performance improvements.

Crediting good intentions or self-realization of an issue (often occurring just prior to the assessment) as the assessment conclusion should be avoided. While such positives can and should be recognized within the business performance assessment report, they must not be allowed to interfere or detract from the real message that performance improvement opportunities do exist and that they should be pursued.

Whether recognized or not, organization leaders accepting assessment report conclusions founded on intention and/or issue self-identification diminish their organization's ability to improve; subsequently slowing its response to internal needs and market

Discovering Business Gold

While not all inclusive, the four lists below, *Process-Based Warning Flags*, *Process Execution Warning Flags - Behaviors*, *Potential, Observable Results*, and *Potential Causes*, are designed to help organization leaders to recognize whether their assessments gloss over the real issues in favor of more positive messages. Only after a problem is recognized and its causes identified can the needed actions be taken to move the organization toward improved performance.

Process-Based Warning Flags

- Guidelines do not exist for the performance of causal analysis
- Business performance assessment program frameworks do not provide for executive or senior management sponsorship each assessment
- Assessment protocols allow for excessive participation by members of the organization being evaluated
- Performance evaluations, merit pay increases, and bonus are overly tied to achievement of high assessment grades/results
- Reward systems do not recognize those performing thorough, value-adding assessments

Process Execution Warning Flags – Behaviors

- Leaders of the evaluated organization interject themselves into the business performance assessment process prior to more senior leaders receiving the report
- Organization leaders have a propensity to 'shoot the messenger' in response to unfavorable news
- Organization leaders do not value constructive criticism and in severe cases may treat delivery of such messages as a career limiting event for the assessment team

---

- Organization leaders actively reward those who routinely present 'good news' and/or the 'desired message'
- Organization leaders do not openly challenge assessment conclusions based on intentions and/or recently self-identified issues
- Organization leaders do not routinely probe for additional information regarding the lower level causes to assessment identified issues and opportunities
- Business performance assessment leaders and team members identifying true improvement opportunities are rebuked by other members of the workforce

Potential, Observable Results

- The organization is slow to react to market changes
- Organization change occurs over long periods of time, typically when a new leader assumes control
- Competitors routinely outperform the organization
- Poor performing employees (delivering softer or the desired messages) advance ahead of stronger performing employees (delivering more accurate but harder messages)
- Poor performing employees (delivering softer or the desired messages) tend to be at least equally compensated and receive similar or greater merit increases and bonuses to stronger performing employees (delivering more accurate but harder messages)
- Better performing employees leave the organization because of its lack of value for strong and improved performance
- Better performing employees admonished for competent performance leading or on an assessment team leave the organization

Discovering Business Gold

Potential Causes

- Executives and managers lack or avoid accountability
- Executives and managers are uncomfortable holding peers and subordinates accountable
- Business performance assessment team leaders and members fear for their job security and so deliver the reports they feel executives and managers will accept without adverse consequences being realized
- The organization's culture does not value constructive feedback as a tool for continuous improvement
- The organization values tenure over performance
- Executives, managers, and the workforce unduly fear the change that comes with organizational improvements

Final Thoughts...

Business performance assessments crediting good intentions or self-identification of issues rarely occur in organizations with a culture that embraces these introspective assessments as a learning opportunity, not a witch hunt. While delivery of the assessment's findings should always be done with respect and tact, no one is served when the message is diluted or hidden.

In addition to avoiding placing a positive spin on one's own self assessments, organizations should watch for similar messaging coming from outsiders such as regulatory organizations and industry groups. If such spin is conveyed in these group's reports, an effort should be made to probe for the underlying issues so to be able to identify the unreported issues.

Effort Bias

Superiors often find it difficult to provide critical feedback to those who put their very heart and soul into their work. Individuals receiving such messages tend to interpret them personally; feeling disappointment, regret, and unappreciated. Rather than constructively improving their performance, these individuals become less productive and contribute substantially less to the organization. Consequently, assessment leaders frequently seek plausible justification to avoid criticizing these individuals' performance; recognizing their exceptional effort while ignoring the results achieved. Doing so, however, foregoes the improvement opportunities and sacrifices the associated gains that could otherwise be realized.

Crediting exceptional effort without correspondingly outstanding results should be avoided. While effort should be recognized, assessment leaders must not be so biased as to allow employees' effort to obscure the identification, documentation, communication, and pursuit of performance improvement opportunities.

Effort biased leaders diminish their organization's ability to improve and, therefore, to remain competitive. While not all inclusive, the four lists below, *Process-Based Warning Flags*, *Process Execution Warning Flags - Behaviors*, *Potential, Observable Results*, and *Potential Causes*, are designed to help organization leaders to recognize whether their assessments preferentially recognize effort over results and forego real performance improvement opportunities. Only after a problem is recognized and its causes identified can the needed actions be taken to move the organization toward improved performance.

Process-Based Warning Flags

- Assessment guidelines drive effort recognition without a corresponding results requirement
- Performance evaluations, merit pay increases, and bonus are overly tied to achievement of high assessment grades/results

Process Execution Warning Flags – Behaviors

- Organization leaders associate value contributed to time spent working rather than actual results achieved
- Managers reward those who appear to be busy
- Executives and managers do not openly challenge assessment conclusions based on effort

Potential, Observable Results

- Work progress tends to remain at 90 percent complete
- Employees take on 'busy-work' and/or seek to 'look busy'
- Competitors routinely outperform the organization
- Better performing employees leave the organization because of its lack of value for superior performance (behaviors plus results)

Potential Causes

- Executives and managers are uncomfortable holding peers and subordinates accountable
- Business performance assessment team leaders fear hurting the feelings of those critiqued
- The organization's culture does not value constructive feedback as a tool for continuous improvement

- The organization values perceived effort over performance (behaviors plus results)

Final Thoughts...

Business performance assessments crediting effort without results rarely occur in organizations with a culture that embraces these introspective assessments as a learning opportunity, not a witch hunt. While delivery of the assessment's findings should always be done with respect and tact, no one is served when the message is diluted or hidden.

In addition to avoiding an effort biased spin in one's own self assessments, leaders should watch for similar messaging coming from external overseers. If such spin is conveyed by these groups, an effort should be made to probe for the underlying causes so to be able to identify and correct the unreported issues.

Conclusion Bias

Business performance assessments can be a powerful tool for determining the unknown drivers of performance; their effectiveness derived from the diverse knowledge and experience of the multidiscipline team and the vast amounts of information from causal evaluations, work performance observations, executive, manager, employee, and customer interviews, financial reports, independent analyst reports, performance measures, and condition reports leveraged to perform these assessments. So rich and robust are these assessments that their credibility often goes unchallenged, yet a single flaw in the assessment's initial execution can make this power tool for continuous improvement an instrument of disaster.

All too often, business performance assessments are used to prove the existence of a conclusion already reached by an organization's leaders. Subsequently, they transform from a truly independent assessment into a fact gathering exercise. Assessment teams directed to evaluate the existence of a given condition often preferentially seek out those facts supporting such a conclusion; intentionally omitting or becoming unintentionally oblivious to those facts supporting a counter argument. Thus, the assessment's outcome is known before it begins and the promise of a deep understanding of actual performance and drivers is forfeit. In these cases, if those commissioning the assessment are not fully correct in their understanding of the associated performance conditions then the assessment's credibility may drive the organization in the wrong direction.

Intended or not, organization leaders specifically directing the performance of business performance assessments to validate a predefined position place at risk the realization of benefits derived from the knowledge of the organization's actual performance and performance drivers. While not all inclusive, the four lists below, *Process-Based Warning Flags*, *Process Execution Warning Flags – Behaviors*, *Potential, Observable Results*, and *Potential Causes*, are designed to help organization leaders to recognize whether their assessments focus on proving preconceived conclusions. Only after a problem is recognized and its causes identified can the needed actions be taken to move the organization toward improved performance.

Process-Based Warning Flags

- Business performance assessment teams report directly to those organization leaders whose area of responsibility is being evaluated (lack of procedure directed independent oversight)
- Business performance assessment process and/or forms call for the identification of conclusions to be focused on early in the process (Note: Identifying categorical areas of focus is acceptable.)

Process Execution Warning Flags – Behaviors

- Executives and senior managers assign business performance assessments to provide the existence of a given condition
- Business performance assessment leaders and teams actively seek to provide a palatable or desired answer to the organization's leadership team
- Business performance assessment interviews and fact finding activities tend to be narrowly focused on a those individuals and facts supporting a desired conclusion
- Business performance assessment team members omit reviewing even significant occurrences that would counter a desired point of view deeming them irrelevant or an anomaly

Potential, Observable Results

- Sustained poor performance when the true root causes of such performance goes unidentified
- A failure to identify and transfer good performance practices from one part of the organization to another resulting in pockets of superior performance and the inability of other workgroups to achieve the same results
- Overall forfeiture of performance potential; maintaining of the status quo and a lack of continuous improvement

Potential Causes

- The organization has a 'shoot the messenger' culture when undesired performance outcomes are identified
- The organization is highly leader driven such that the workforce to often seeks to please leaders; providing them with the information and conclusions they believe the leaders want to receive
- A lack of training and understanding of the assessment process and the principles behind performance of high quality, insightful assessments
- Desire on the part of the leader commissioning the assessment to use this tool as a method of mitigation or, in extreme cases, cover up personal performance shortfalls
- An inappropriate expression of a leader's desire to move the organization in a particular direction

Final Thought...

Business performance assessments seeking to prove a predetermined conclusion, particularly one that is negative will appear to those whose performance evaluated as being grossly unfair. Subsequently, these individuals tend to resist the assessment's conclusions even if they are based on solid facts and sound reasoning. This lack of buy-in results in a lack of support for the identified improvement initiatives. Worse still, the feelings of unfairness create disenfranchisement that drives lower productivity and possible attrition.

Content Without Context

"Don't make a mountain out of a mole hill."

Author Unknown

Because all things are relative, context is important. All too often, individuals react to a given set of circumstances or facts without considering the context within which those circumstances or facts exist. Consequently, the importance assigned to the circumstances or facts may exceed that which is warranted.

Applying context during an assessment is extremely important. Without context, an assessment team may inappropriately identify issues and recommend corrective actions that are themselves more costly to implement than the savings to be gained by the issue's resolution. Similarly, the assessment team itself may spend more money identifying and developing an issue than the value potential presented by implementing the performance improvement.

Business performance assessment team leaders and members asserting the existence of issues and recommending corrective actions without the proper context can cause serious harm to an organization. Such action greatly diminishes the assessment's value; robbing the organization of opportunities to improve. While not all inclusive, the four lists below, *Process-Based Warning Flags*, *Process Execution Warning Flags - Behaviors*, *Potential, Observable Results*, and *Potential Causes*, provide insight as to whether assessment findings contain the context necessary to ensure their relevancy. Only after a problem is recognized and its causes identified can the needed actions be taken to move the organization toward improved performance.

Process-Based Warning Flags

- Assessment procedures exclude participation of local personnel
- Evaluation processes do not require a findings briefing for managers of the organization being assessed prior to final report issuance
- Assessment guidelines preclude the use of external assessors
- Evaluation methods do not include the use of common tools that help provide contextual references such as Pareto Analysis, Performance Models, Process Flowcharts, etcetera
- Programs gathering, analyzing, and processing internal and external benchmark data are immature or do not exist

Process Execution Warning Flags – Behaviors

- Assessors ignore the input provided by local personnel
- Evaluators do not reference outside benchmarks or emphatically reference only their own experience
- Assessors do not consider unique circumstances that necessarily drive the cited performance
- Evaluators are closed to considering approaches outside of their experience base
- Assessors do not consider the interactions between processes, functions, and equipment

Potential, Observable Results

- Assessed managers and staff become disenfranchised with the business performance assessment process; participating less and resisting the implementation of _all_ recommended solutions

---

- Creativity and innovation is stifled, particularly when such changes upset the status quo (even though overall results may be significantly improved)
- Distrust builds between individuals and work groups grows because of the assessors apparent lack of openness to new and/or different ideas
- Cross-functional coordination and support within the organization is weak diminishing the organization's ability to deliver products, services, and initiatives requiring broad participation
- Organizational results - operational performance improvements, market share gains, revenue growth, etcetera - lag that of competitors and the economy in general

Potential Causes

- Common evaluation methods, models, and tools, do not exist, are immature, or not used
- Assessors are not trained in evaluation processes including the use of analytical models and evaluation tools
- Assessors have not been trained and/or are not knowledgeable of the interactions between processes, functions, and equipment
- Organization leaders, managers, and employees do not value external experience
- Individuals are closed to new and/or different ideas - *if it was not invented here, it shouldn't be done* culture
- Divisions within the organization operate in a highly siloed fashion

Identifying Mostly Strengths

All organizations, including the best of the best, have room for improvement and those not improving inevitably find themselves falling behind competitors. Self-critical evaluations are therefore critical to achieving continuous performance improvement and remaining competitive. Evaluations identifying mostly strengths offer little opportunity for organizational growth.

Most executives, managers, and employees take personal and professional pride in their organization; after all, they commit a significant portion of their lives to their place of work and often form significant personal relationships with colleagues. During assessments, this pride may cloud evaluators' judgment resulting in a less than critical examination of performance and the more prevalent identification of strengths than opportunities for improvement.

Performance strengths are significantly easier to identify than opportunities for improvement. First, there is little need to determine the 'three whys deep' drivers of positive performance, the immediate driver is typically all that is needed for broad-based replication. Second, assessors need not be as familiar with specific, comparable internal and external benchmark methods; recognizing positive performance results relative to that of other internal organizations or that of the market in general. Third, evaluators forego the need to deliver an undesirable message to superiors, peers, and subordinates. Identifying mostly strengths during assessments is typically a disservice to the organization. Such reports are developed through the expenditure of precious organizational resources without a commensurate return on investment. While not all inclusive, the four lists below, *Process-Based Warning Flags*, *Process Execution Warning Flags - Behaviors*, *Potential*, *Observable Results*, and *Potential Causes*, are designed to help organization leaders to recognize when their assessments lack objective criticality. Only after a problem is recognized and its causes identified can the needed actions be taken to move the organization toward improved performance.

Process-Based Warning Flags

- Assessment guidelines do not specify some target number of issues or ratio of issues to strengths to be identified
- Business performance assessment participants do not receive qualification training on the performance of critical observations, interviews, and data analysis
- Performance evaluations, merit pay increases, and bonus are overly tied to achievement of high assessment grades/results

Process Execution Warning Flags – Behaviors

- Organization leaders accept reported performance strengths with little or no challenge
- Leaders aggressively challenge the performance improvement findings returned by assessment teams
- Executives and managers do not openly challenge assessment reports containing an elevated number of strengths or high strength to finding ratio
- Assessment leaders are eager to deliver a positive message but hesitate to present a critical one

Potential, Observable Results

- Business performance assessment reports contain an excessively high number of strengths relative to performance improvement opportunity findings
- Organizational performance improves at a slow rate
- Competitors routinely outperform the organization

Potential Causes

- Executives and managers are uncomfortable holding peers and subordinates accountable
- Pride clouded judgment of assessment leaders and team members
- Evaluation team leaders and members lack the industry knowledge and experience necessary to perform critical assessments
- Assessment team leaders resist or are uncomfortable conveying difficult performance improvement messages
- The organization's culture does not value constructive feedback as a tool for continuous improvement

Acronyms

BPA: Business Performance Assessment

FA: Functional area

IOBPAC: Individual Organization Business Process Assessment Calendar

SMART: Specific, Measurable, Achievable, Realistic, and Time-bound

Glossary

Business Performance Assessment: evaluation of one's own performance focused on the associated dimensions of people, process, and technology.

Business Performance Assessment Summary: an analysis report issued by Functional Area Managers documenting the common performance issues, repeat findings, trends identified through collective evaluation of functional area business performance assessment reports.

Best Practices: Those activities or performance attributes that enhance organizational results. Best practices may be procedurally driven or behaviorally based. Consequently, best practices can be readily observed, recognized, and quantified.

Control Processes: Those processes that manage the Operational and Infrastructure processes. (i.e. Goal Setting, Performance Monitoring)

Event-based Assessments: assessments performed after a significant performance expectation violation that sets a dangerous precedent or causes significantly adverse impacts to the organization. The assessments scans a broad number of organizational groups, especially those performing similar operations to that group in which the violation occurred, so to identify the extent of condition of the undesired deviation and to broadly reinforce adherence to proper management standards. Note that the business performance assessment and corrective action programs should also be examined to determine why precursor deviations were not identified and corrective action taken prior to the event's occurrence

Foundational Assessments: assessments occurring at a given frequency within a defined time interval typically focused on core business risks, operational goals, and organizational values. These assessments target those critical organizational functions and characteristics which present significant risk, must be performed with precision, or require continuous improvement to maintain marketplace competitiveness

Horizontal Cut Assessment: often referred to as a mile-wide and an inch deep, these business performance assessments focused on numerous performances of a single activity performed by a broad range of organizational workgroups

Infrastructure Processes: Those processes that support the Operational processes. (i.e. Human Resource Management, Finance)

Master Business Performance Assessment Calendar: integrated, date-based representation of an organization's business performance assessment portfolio

Observations: an ongoing business performance assessment activity, performance-based observation and critical evaluation of ongoing activities on a regular basis by knowledgeable personnel.

Operational Processes: Those processes related directly to achievement of the organization's mission. These processes guide the creation of products and provision of services that generate the organization's output. (i.e. Production / Operations Management, Work Management)

Principles: Fundamental activities or performance attributes without which effective performance cannot be achieved. Principles may be embedded within procedures or behavioral standards/expectations. Consequently, principle-based activities or performance should be readily observable.

Process: A process is a series of actions and decisions used to transform raw inputs into a desired output.

Random Assessments: assessments reinforcing desired behaviors performed at the discretion of the business performance assessment program manager and/or senior organization leaders.   Such random assessments reinforce with employees the need to be ever vigilant to the adherence of workplace standards because their compliance is monitored at all times

Situational Assessments: assessments targeted at specific high-risk activities to ensure risk mitigating behaviors and mechanisms are present during these critical times. These assessments include reviews of the integrated training, execution, and follow-up improvements associated with these events

Vertical Slice Assessment: often referred to as an inch-wide and a mile deep, these business performance assessments evaluate all transactions and organizational transitions as a process is executed from initiation to planning, scheduling, execution, and final closure

Warning Flags: Those activities or performance attributes that diminish an organization's effectiveness. By their very nature, warning flags are active, not passive. They may be procedurally driven or behaviorally based. Consequently, warning flags can be readily observed, recognized, and corrected or eliminated.

References

Internal Control – Integrated Framework, Committee of Sponsoring Organizations of the Treadway Commission (COSO), May 2013

ISO 31000 – Risk Management, International Organization for Standardization, 2009

Project Management Body of Knowledge – Fifth Edition, Project Management Institute, 2013

Additional Resources

Sevian Business Performance Assessment Program

Implement the turnkey program that drives excellence in every aspect of your business's performance. *In 2014 alone, Sevian Business Performance Assessments identified over $200 million of performance improvement opportunities across four companies!* **Just imagine what it might do for you.** [1]

Business performance assessments represent in-depth evaluations of organizational functions for the purpose of identifying improvement opportunities. The Sevian Business Performance Assessment Program provides all of the tools and information needed to establish a robust, best practice assessment program guiding objective evaluation of organizational performance.

A Fully Developed, Immediately Implementable Business Performance Assessment Program

Implemented by Fortune 500, large regional, and small companies, the Sevian Business Performance Assessment Program contains all of the components necessary to implement a fully mature assessment program on day one - *truly enabling turnkey performance excellence.* Each program package includes:

- ▪ *Program Introduction*: establishes the framework for immediate program implementation, effective execution, and long-term governance.

- ***Program Maturity Model***: defines the progression of several key program characteristics, differentiating between those organizations achieving minimalist results and others optimizing the strategic value of their efforts.

- ***Program Flowcharts and Activity Basis***: provides the detailed underlying stakeholder, input, process, output, and customer information necessary for effective program governance as well as supporting software application implementation.

- ***Process Procedure***: detailed step-by-step assessment performance instructions that are fully human factored to ensure consistent, accurate, program execution. The procedure also includes all models, forms, and templates needed to successfully perform value-adding assessments.

- ***Program Execution Guides***: provide detailed information on how to optimally perform major assessment activities.

- ***Form Use Instructional Guides***: provide step-by-step instructions on how to use and complete each process form.

- ***Model Use Instructional Guides***: provide step-by-step instructions on the application and use of each process model.

- ***Program Principles, Best Practices, and Warning Flags***: elaborate on those core elements necessary for consistently superior program and process performance and highlight those practices and behaviors that should be avoided so to optimize program value.

To further support Sevian Business Performance Assessment Program implementation, StrategyDriven offers classroom-based program introductory training and initial assessment facilitation.

For information on how to acquire the Sevian Business Performance Assessment Program, assessment training, and facilitated assessment support, contact us at Products@StrategyDriven.com or visit our website at www.StrategyDriven.com/BPAP.

Sevian Business Performance Assessment Program Guides and Forms

Sevian Business Performance Assessment Program Guides and Forms incorporate *Discovering Business Gold*'s principles and best practices (and avoid the warning flags) to enhance specific aspects of your assessment program.

Guides

Sevian Business Performance Assessment Program Guides provide detailed how-to activity instructions accompanied by the associated forms and form instructions. Available guides include:

- Kick-off Meeting Guide
- Observation Guide
- Periodic Functional Area Manager Briefing Guide
- Dealing with Difficult Functional Area Managers Guide
- Beneficial Practices Development Guide
- Performance Shortfall Development Guide
- Overall Performance Determination Guide
- Exit Meeting Guide

To learn more and purchase Sevian Business Performance Assessment Guides visit www.StrategyDriven.com/BPAPGuides.

Forms

Sevian Business Performance Assessment Program Forms provide ready-to-use templates to document every aspect of the assessment process. Each form is accompanied by a step-by-step instructional guide detailing the form's completion. Available forms include:

- Scope and Approach Development Form
- Team Leader / Team Member Selection Form
- Team Leader Checklist Form
- Business Performance Assessment Notification Form
- Business Performance Assessment Data Request Form
- Assessment Planning Form
- Assessment Schedule Form
- Kickoff Meeting Briefing Form
- Business Performance Assessment Observation Form
- Periodic Briefing Outline Form
- Business Performance Assessment Objective / Criteria Confirmation Form
- Beneficial Practice Development Form
- Shortfall Development Form
- Business Performance Assessment Report Form
- Exit Meeting Briefing Form
- Team Leader Performance Grading Form
- Team Member Performance Grading Form
- Business Performance Assessment Performance Grading Form
- Assessment Closeout Form
- Business Performance Assessment Program Performance Grading Form

To learn more and purchase Sevian Business Performance Assessment Forms visit www.StrategyDriven.com/BPAPForms.

StrategyDriven Business Performance Assessment Program Forum

An organization's business performance assessment program plays a key role in identifying the performance improvement opportunities that will propel it to the next level of performance. Articles, podcasts, documents, and other resources contained in the StrategyDriven Business Performance Assessment Forum explore the leading practices of companies successfully executing an assessment program in support of strategic business planning and tactical business execution.

Visit the StrategyDriven Business Performance Assessment Forum at: www.StrategyDriven.com/BPAPForum

---

1. Results will vary and are not guaranteed. Performance improvement opportunities listed are atypical and may not be available within some organizations or assessment areas. Additionally, these performance improvement opportunities were identified during business performance assessments led and performed by StrategyDriven Advisors possessing specific technical knowledge of and experience in the assessed areas.

Related Programs

Surviving and thriving in today's rapidly changing market requires organizational agility and the means to make rapid and sound decisions. Both of these activities require high quality and timely information on the performance of the internal organization and the many factors of its external market environment.

Performance monitoring involves the acquisition of important data followed by its consolidation and interpretation into useful information. It is from this information that leaders can identify internal performance improvement opportunities, monitor progress toward achieving goals, and identify marketplace shifts providing opportunities and threats to the organization.

Materials in StrategyDriven's Monitoring forums explore the principles, best practices, and warning flags associated with effective performance monitoring programs including:

StrategyDriven Evaluation & Control Program Forum – Evaluation and control program components play a key role in an organization's learning and growth efforts. They not only identify improvement opportunities, they also identify internal and external best practices that can be used to better existing processes. This continuous growth mechanism is critical to an organization seeking to maintain and advance its position in the marketplace.

StrategyDriven Management Observation Program Forum – Lasting individual and organization performance improvement occurs through ongoing reinforcement of desired individual and group behaviors, modification of counterproductive behaviors, and elimination of organizational barriers to performance excellence. A well designed and executed management observation program serves as an effective performance improvement and reinforcement tool to achieve these long-term performance changes.

StrategyDriven Organizational Performance Measures Forum – Performance measures serve to align an organization's efforts to the achievement of its mission. As part of a company's evaluation and control program, they quantifiably monitor important characteristics of the company's products and services and the performance of the individuals and processes creating them.

All three of these performance improvement forums can be access from the StrategyDriven website at: www.StrategyDriven.com/Monitoring.

About the Author

Nathan Ives MBA, PMP
President & CEO
StrategyDriven Enterprises, LLC

Nathan Ives is a highly successful executive with over twenty years of Energy Industry and consulting experience. As an experienced management consultant, he serves as a trusted advisor to executives and senior managers at dozens of Fortune 500, government, and large regional companies; helping them define organizational needs and develop and manage the complex, mission critical projects needed to improve operational effectiveness and lower costs. In this role, he leads teams of experienced utility professionals in the design and implementation of integrated fleet asset management processes including strategic asset and resource planning, online and outage work management, engineering change and configuration management, document and records management, and corrective action programs. Nathan's insights have been quoted by news journalists, published in several well respected periodicals, presented at national conferences, and broadcast internationally via webcast.

Prior to becoming a management consultant, Nathan held several influential nuclear industry positions at the Institute of Nuclear Power Operations (INPO). During his tenure, he led teams of nuclear operations professionals in the performance evaluation of over 24 nuclear electric generating stations from 20 utilities in the United States, Canada, and Japan. He also led the nuclear industry's effort to redefine performance standards in the areas of organizational alignment, managerial decision-making, plant operations, and risk management; authoring or significantly contributing to several publications against which nuclear power plant performance is evaluated.

Nathan attended the United States Naval Academy in Annapolis, Maryland; earning a Bachelor of Science degree in physics. He later received a master of business administration degree from Kennesaw State University and was elected to membership in the Beta Gamma Sigma and Phi Kappa Phi honor societies.

Nathan served on the Nuclear Energy Institute's New Nuclear Plant Executive Taskforce and the Graduate Student Advisory Board at Kennesaw State University's Coles College of Business. He is a member of the Project Management Institute and the American Management Association.

About StrategyDriven

StrategyDriven provides executives and managers with the planning and execution advice, tools, and practices needed to create greater organizational alignment and accountability for the achievement of superior results. We believe a clear, forward-looking strategy, translatable to the day-to-day activities of all organization members, is critical to realizing success in today's fast paced market environment. Not only does a compelling, well-executed strategy align individuals to common goals, it ensures those goals best serve the company's mission.

At StrategyDriven, our seasoned business leaders deliver real-world strategic business planning and tactical execution best practice advice – a blending of workplace experience with sound research and academic principles – to business leaders who may not otherwise have access to these resources.

StrategyDriven refers to the family of organizations comprising StrategyDriven Enterprises, LLC. For more information, please visit www.StrategyDriven.com.